NO MORE LIMITS
TO YOUR
destiny

FERDINARD S LAWSON

NO MORE LIMITS TO YOUR *destiny*

MEMOIRS
Cirencester

Published by Memoirs

MEMOIRS
PUBLISHING

Memoirs Books
25 Market Place, Cirencester, Gloucestershire, GL7 2NX
info@memoirsbooks.co.uk www.memoirspublishing.com

Copyright ©Ferdinard S Lawson, May 2012
First published in England, May 2012
Book jacket design Ray Lipscombe

ISBN 978-1-909020-41-2

All rights reserved.

No part of this publication may be reproduced, stored in a retrieval system, or transmitted in any form or by any means, electronic, mechanical, photocopying, recording or otherwise without the prior permission of Memoirs.

Although the author and publisher have made every effort to ensure that the information in this book was correct when going to press, we do not assume and hereby disclaim any liability to any party for any loss, damage, or disruption caused by errors or omissions, whether such errors or omissions result from negligence, accident, or any other cause. The views expressed in this book are purely the author's.

Printed in England

NO MORE LIMITS TO YOUR *destiny*

CONTENTS

ABOUT THIS BOOK
ABOUT THE AUTHOR
DEDICATION
ACKNOWLEDGEMENTS
INTRODUCTION

Chapter 1	RENEWING YOUR MIND	Page 1
Chapter 2	DON'T BURY YOUR TALENT	Page 8
Chapter 3	LEARNING NOT TO PUT THINGS OFF	Page 15
Chapter 4	STAYING AWAY FROM TOXIC RELATIONSHIPS	Page 31
Chapter 5	STANDING FIRM ON YOUR PURPOSE IN LIFE	Page 40
Chapter 6	THE POWER OF PRAYER IN YOUR LIFE	Page 49
Chapter 7	GET RID OF NEGATIVE THOUGHTS	Page 57
Chapter 8	PURSUE, OVERTAKE AND RECOVER YOUR DESTINY	Page 68
Chapter 9	TRUST IN THE LORD	Page 86
Chapter 10	WALK BY FAITH	Page 90
Chapter 11	DEVELOPING THE ATTITUDE OF GRATITUDE	Page 97
	CONCLUSION	Page 109
	BIBLIOGRAPHY	Page 112

FERDINARD S LAWSON

NO MORE LIMITS TO YOUR *destiny*

How to live your life to the full and
how to fulfil your true destiny

ABOUT THIS BOOK

What is limiting your progress in life?

Almighty God created each and every one of us and He has given us the power to have dominion over all things within our capability. He has a definite purpose and plan for your life and that includes rising above all the limitations of your life (DESTINY).

No problem has ever come to stay, and none will ever stay in your life when you discover what to do with the word of God. Are you being limited by your past mistakes, relationships, family curses or evil pronouncements? Perhaps you are experiencing injustice, mistreatment or ill-treatment, abuse from work or oppression that is threatening your destiny. The word of God breaks all barriers and limitations. KNOW THAT YOUR GOD IS UNLIMITED - AND SO ARE YOU.

Embark on the journey of knowing that the power of God that created the whole universe empowers you to rise above all things. You will be unstoppable and unlimited as you pursue, overtake and recover all that you are destined for. There will be 'no more limits to your destiny'.

ABOUT THE AUTHOR

Ferdinard Senyo Lawson is a warm and dynamic Christian who enjoys serving God and the men of God. He became a Born-Again Christian while in the Deeper Life Bible Church in Ghana, where he served as Youth Leader within the Youth Praise and Worship Team, so in his position as a House Fellowship Leader, Ferdinand took delight in encouraging and motivating young believers to remain focused in serving the Lord.

As a former student of Oda Secondary School (ODASCO) in Ghana, he also served as the Assistant House Prefect, and was involved in several Scripture Union activities. He was seen as one of the finest and most disciplined students of his time.

Ferdinard's mandate is to empower, motivate and encourage believers to remain focused in serving the Lord. Ferdinard's passion for services to the Lord including his loyalty in the area of serving men of God is unparalleled; particularly regarding his current worship and service in the House of Judah (Praise) Ministries in the United Kingdom. He serves as the armour bearer to Bishop Michael Hutton-Wood, Senior Pastor of House of Judah (Praise) Ministries.

Ferdinand now lives in London (UK) with his wife Deborah and their two lovely children, Prince Joshua and Princess Jessica.

DEDICATION

I dedicate this book to all men and women who in the past were limited and never given a chance in society but through the word of God now have a successful and effective life.

I would like to express my appreciation of my parents, especially my father, Mr Marcus Chris Agbeko Lawson, for being a great and lovely father. I would also like to thank all other members of my family for the care and love they have shown me during my formative years. Finally, I want to express my gratitude to my wife and children for their support.

God bless you all.

ACKNOWLEDGEMENTS

I give all glory to the Lord God Almighty for revealing himself to me and given me his word to share with this generation and the generation unborn. It is an opportunity to contribute to what other men of God have written through experience to encourage the body of Christ.

My sincere thanks goes to my destiny father, Bishop Michael Hutton-Wood and his wife (Rev. Bernice A. Hutton-Wood), who themselves are writers, and the Senior Pastors of the House of Judah Praise Ministry with the mandate to raise generational leaders to impact nations, by empowering men and women to release their full potential to maximize their destiny. God bless you for believing in us that we can all fulfill our destiny. You never gave up on anybody but kept preaching the word of God to us. Thank you for your input into my personal life.

I express my profound gratitude to my spiritual mentor, pastor Charles Owusu of the Deeper Christian Life Bible Church Ghana, for being an inspiration and a life coach to me. God bless you.

Finally I thank all brothers and sisters in the body of Christ, especially the members of House of Judah Praise Ministry for their unfailing prayers.

May God increase you all.

INTRODUCTION

YOUR DISABILITY REVEALS YOUR ABILITIES

Limitations are any conditions that restrict an individual from getting from one point to another. They can also be regarded as a form of weakness, lack of capacity, or an inability or handicap which prevents you achieving something. Limitations comes in different forms and shapes to an individual. This can be in the form of lack of educational knowledge, inability to bear children or lack of capacity to retain material or information.

Limitations are any form of rules, situations and circumstances that prevent free movement. They may also be any form of condition that limits an individual's ability to improve, due to a defect, a failing and/or shortfall. Limitations may come in many forms; some may be imposed by others, some by misconceptions, while others may be self-imposed. Limitations may sometimes exist purely because of our own individual perspectives about life's circumstances.

The life of Jabez in 1 Chronicles 4:-9-10 is a typical example of limitation. The Bible gave an account that he was more honourable than his brothers, even though his mother had named him Jabez, meaning sorrow, suffering and pain. We saw here that his mother placed a limitation on him. This however, affected his life until one day he discovered that he had to do something about these limitations on his destiny. He also understood that it does not really matter what family background he came from, but if he could discover himself through the word of God and what God had put in him, he would definitely get to his destiny in life.

'The future is what you make it and not what you think it should be, but is created by those who turn adversity into advantage and do not allow their past to hold their life hostage'
Bishop Michael Hutton-Wood

When you face things or situations and think that they are beyond your abilities or capacity to deal with, it is an issue. Amazingly, these are the very things you are supposed to do to bring the best out of you. Moses had been chosen to deliver the Jewish people from the slavery of the Pharaoh and the cruel Egyptians. God saw the potential in Moses but Moses was looking at his limitation - an inability to speak.

The Bible explained in Exodus 1:1-6 that Moses had had a speech impediment since he was a child which made it impossible for him to speak out or communicate the very Word the Lord God had given to His people. He was consumed by his inability to speak, and the Bible says he was giving reason as to why he could not go and save God's people: *'I am no man of words, heavy of mouth and heavy of speech.'*

In addition, Moses felt that saving the children of Israel was too big for him to embark upon due to his limitation. Sometimes you need to see beyond your limitation to life and see how God sees you. He created you in his image and the Bible says *'For I know the thoughts that I think toward you, saith the LORD, thoughts of peace, and not of evil, to give you an expected end'* - **Jeremiah 29: 11.**

'Before I formed thee in the belly I knew thee; and before thou camest forth out of the womb I sanctified thee, and I ordained thee a prophet unto the nations' - **Jeremiah 1:5**

Therefore in the case of Moses, God himself had to reassure him that He, God, had created him and given him the mouth he was complaining about. God gave Moses the enablement, courage and strength to overcome his limitations.

'And we know that all things work together for good to them that love God, to them who are the called according to his purpose' - **Romans 8:28.**

God has a purpose for your life and the gate of hell cannot stop you from achieving your desired destiny or future. We saw in the life of Hannah, the wife of Elkanah, who the Bible said was barren and sometimes mocked by Peninnah, her rival. It came to pass in her life as she went up to worship in Shiloh. The Bible gave an account that Hannah cried before the Lord and made a vow to the Lord God almighty that if He the Lord would give her a son, she would give him back to God.

The Lord God answered Hannah's cry and gave her a son. God heard Hannah's weeping and turned it into joy. He is still in the business of turning our weeping into joy. He did the same for Joseph. One night Joseph was in prison, the next day he was in the palace. God has not changed. What He did for Hannah and Joseph, He can do for you.

We must also realize that the Bible says in Luke 1:37, *'For nothing is impossible for God.'* He can heal our bodies and our minds and even change the events of our life, for nothing is impossible for Him. There are so many places in the Bible where God actually changed the past. His thoughts are above our thoughts, his love we can grow in, but never grasp fully. He desires to fill us with his fullness and to get us out of the way of limitations and failures, as it is not his wish that these shortfalls become our lot. God's unlimited blessings are also reflected in 2 Kings 4:6: *'And it came to pass, when the vessels were full, that she said unto her son, bring me another vessel. And he said unto her, there is not a vessel more, and the oil ceased.'*

'Limitations live only in our minds, but if we use our imaginations our possibilities become limitless' - **Jamie Paolinetti**

So long as there were vessels to be filled, the miraculous flow of oil continued. It ceased only when there were no more jars to contain it. The lady had just enough vessels to contain the flow of oil, thus she had limited vessels when God had an unlimited flow of oil of blessings to change her life and that of her entire generation.

From the account she had the opportunity to go and borrow extra vessels, but made the choice to limit the prophet, who did not speak any word to stop the flow of the oil. This is to say that our readiness to allow God to expand our limited ideas, vessels, nets and indeed our coast in making impact can only be made possible if we stop limiting the power of God. No limitation is above God and we cannot fail in life, as no amount of limitation under the universe can restrain the blessings of God in our lives.

Peter was discouraged because of his own failure (limitation). After he denied the Lord three times, Peter went out and wept bitterly, we are told. I imagine he felt that he had blown it for good, and he must have been terribly discouraged with himself. How could he deny the Lord, the one he promised never to deny?

'And he said unto me, my grace is sufficient for thee: for my strength is made perfect in weakness. Most gladly therefore will I rather glory in my infirmities, that the power of Christ may rest upon me' - **2 Corinthians 12:9.**

No limitation is above God and therefore you cannot fail in life, as no amount of limitation in the universe can restrain the blessings of God in our lives. As you read this book may God empower you to overcome every form of limitation standing before your destiny. May you see the treasure in you and not the trash around you. Be blessed as you read on.

CHAPTER ONE

RENEWING YOUR MIND

'And do not be conformed to this world, but be transformed by the renewing of your mind, that you may prove what is that good and acceptable and perfect will of God.'- **Romans 12:2.**

Renewing an individuals mind is very important in producing great transformation and impact. Our mind is the powerhouse to success or failure in life. That is why the Bible teaches us to renew our mind daily, because that is the only way of being acceptable in society and in the will of God. When your mind is renewed you are able to prove yourself in the things of God and able to live in the will of God designed for you.

Nancy Missler once said in her book 'Be Ye Transformed' that renewing our minds is not simply changing our thoughts, but actually putting off the old, negative thoughts as well as putting on God's thoughts. In other words we cannot just say to God, 'Lord, give me Your thoughts' and somehow expect Him to automatically give us His mind. We must first put off our own self-centred thinking by confessing, repenting and then giving it to God. At this point, we can then put on the Mind of Christ.

CHAPTER ONE

Therefore it is possible to say that a renewed mind is putting put off any sin (any hurt, doubt, fear, rebellion, self-centredness, lust, bitterness, etc.), any corrupt thinking or any barrier that would quench God's Spirit and has 'put on' the Mind of Christ (2 Corinthians 10:5).

Apostle Paul again exhorted us believers, mentioned in Ephesians 4:22-24, to put off or do away with the former conversation (behaviour), the old man (old self), which is corrupt according to the deceitful lusts, and be renewed in the spirit of your mind; and that ye put on the new man (the new self), which after God is created in righteousness and true holiness.

'The secret of your future is hidden in your daily routine therefore be careful about what occupies your mind because it will greatly determine what you will become tomorrow''- **Bishop Michael Hutton - Wood.**

Our minds control our thoughts. Your mind tells your body exactly what to do, create, invest in and what not do at a particular given time of the year. That is why it is vital that you renew your mindset each day with God's word against bad memory, depressive feeling, and everything that takes your focus off Him. We renew a lot of things we use in our everyday lives. Amazingly, each and every one us renews our car insurance and our home insurance, while some of us embrace very conscious methods when it comes to renewing it. Any sensible and forward-moving government of any

CHAPTER ONE

country may want to update or renew policies that are not working relating to any socio-economical situation of the country. For example, the UK Government reforming the National Health Service, the welfare states and other financial policies in order to restructure the economy and to maintain relationship in the global market.

'Attitude determines one's Altitude' - **Bishop David Oyedepo Snr**

We use our minds by thinking. Therefore your life today is a result of what you thought about yesterday. It is very important that we really watch what goes through our minds especially the negative experiences that keep coming into our minds, and take control of it by renewing it daily.

In discussing how to negotiate your desired future with today's currency, Bishop Michael Hutton-Wood explained that the best way to deal with and forget about your negative experiences is to become fruitful and occupy yourself with productive thinking to produce something positive to impact nations.

Renewing your mind with the word of God concerning your destiny gives you assurance which then promotes your confidence in your ability to pursue great things in life. It does not matter if you have experienced failures and shortcoming. When you begin to renew your mindset by changing the way you see yourself, you can embark on the road to achievement.

'He who controls the past controls the future' - **George Orwell, 1984.**

CHAPTER ONE

In his book *Think like a Winner*, Dr. Walter Staples writes 'The key to success lies in your particular manner of thinking. When you change how you think about yourself, your relationships, your goals, and your world, your life changes'. If you change the quality of your thinking, you necessarily will change the quality of your life and overcome every form of limitation limiting your destiny.

Your life today is a result of what you thought about yesterday. Therefore your happiness depends primarily on your attitude in life, and especially on the nature and quality of your thoughts, which are more powerful than you may imagine. The world is what you think it is. If you think it is bad, you won't be able to make progress. Your thoughts influence your existence, as well as your environment. You'll be happy or unhappy depending on whether your thoughts are positive or negative. To make your ideas as powerful as possible, they have to be positive. When a negative idea enters your mind, use the sure word of God to get rid of it.

'The man who views the world at fifty the same as he did at twenty has wasted thirty years of his life.' **Muhammad Ali**

Remember that in life, relationships do not last forever. Therefore it is very important that when people leave your life, you do not get angry, bitter or regretful. Just motivate yourself to do better than when they left you. Whatever the case you are more precious to your generation than people think you are.

CHAPTER ONE

Your chosen dream (vision, purpose, and goal) demands the right environment or climate to materialize. It is vital that you control your environment or the atmosphere around your dream or that atmosphere will definitely control you. This is to say that the individual climate we create knowingly or unknowingly determines and influences our behaviour and the decisions we make.

It does not matter what environment you grew up in. As long as you are prepared and ready to change a negative atmosphere with the word of God, then you can be assured that you are making progress.

Nobody else can create your atmosphere for you - **Mike Murdock.**

What you see and how you see it controls your mind and your desire. If you see yourself as great and powerful, then you will do the right things to bring those dreams to pass in your life. Therefore do not sit down and wait for somebody else to make things happen for you. You have to take control of what goes into your mind.

Begin to invest in your future and the environment that inspires you towards excellence and the improvement of your life. Our thoughts influence our existence, as well as our environment. Your happiness or unhappiness depends on whether your thoughts are reformed or deformed in a particular situation.

CHAPTER ONE

'In whatever position you find yourself, determine first your objective.' - **Ferdinand Foch, French Army Marshall**

Proverbs 23:7 says: *'As a man thinks in his heart, so is he'*. You cannot have a happy life if you have a sad mind. You need a healthy mind to start with. Your mind is the one that makes you the person God made you to be.

Charles Stanley once said 'renewing the mind is a little like refinishing furniture'. He explained that it is a two-stage process which involves taking off the old and replacing it with the new. The old is the lies you have learned to tell or were taught by those around you; it is the attitudes and ideas that have become a part of your thinking but do not reflect reality. The new is the truth. To renew your mind is to involve yourself in the process of allowing God to bring to the surface the lies you have mistakenly accepted, and replace them with truth.

In the journey to your destiny, there will be various limitations that will face you along the way to change your direction to that destiny. The good news is that as you begin to renew your mind of those negatives and limited situations which are preventing you from getting to your destiny with the word of God, you will overcome your limitations in Jesus' Name. The hand of God is upon you as it was on Ezekiel when he came across the valley full of dried bones.

If you want to make your life a success, you already have everything you need inside you. You don't have to go looking anywhere else. If you want information about something, it's natural to look for it in exterior sources like books, TV and radio, the Internet, expert opinions, and so on.

If you want to make your life a success, you shouldn't look to the outside but seek solutions inside yourself, because the spirit of God dwells in you. He is ready to reveal your real self to you. We all have personal qualities we express in our own way. They belong only to us, no one else. Discovering them is the most wonderful adventure that exists for human beings, and it always leads to great success. Spend a few minutes every day reflecting on your own possibilities, not your disabilities. Sit down comfortably in a quiet place, keeping your back straight.

Try to find somewhere isolated where you won't be disturbed. Turn your gaze inward, and sincerely ask the Holy Spirit to reveal your true abilities. Then think about how you can develop them. This process is infallible. Observe the thoughts that flow through your mind as you concentrate on your request. With time and patience, you'll find everything you need to lead the life of your dreams. No more limits to your destiny.

CHAPTER TWO

DON'T BURY YOUR TALENT

Burying something means disposing, hiding away or covering with earth. In this context, I am referring to how not to dispose, hide away or cover gifts and talents that God had endowed in you before you were born.

Gift and talent are not limited only to what you are good at. The passion or desire to accomplish that particular thing in life regardless of limitations gives you fulfillment and happiness. Any gift or talent that does not bring you fulfillment in life is actually not your gift or talent.

The Merriam-Webster online dictionary defines talent as 'a characteristic feature, aptitude, or disposition of a person, the natural endowments of a person and a special often athletic, creative, or artistic aptitude'.

We sometimes limit ourselves in many ways, which makes it impossible to appreciate the importance of the gifts and talent God has created us with. This might even tempt you to hide your talent. The question here is, why do people hide or bury their talent in the first place? I have discovered that it may be because of fear of failure. This can be a limitation to your destiny.

The Bible says in **Deuteronomy 31:8** that God *'will not fail or forsake you. Do not fear or be dismayed'*. And in **Romans 12:6** *'In his grace, God has given us different gifts for doing certain things well. So if God has given you the ability to prophesy, speak out with as much faith as God has given you'*.

Fear places limitations in your life and hinders you from getting to your desired future. The devil uses your limitations to move you away from focusing on God's word concerning you. Do not limit yourself from getting to your destiny. Whatever gift or talent you have, begin to take the step of faith and do something with that talent and you will see the salvation of God in your life.

'A gift unrewarded is a gift unused' - **Unknown**

Don't lose your enthusiasm about how to use your talent, do not bury that gift in you or hide it because of what people might have said concerning it. It does not matter what you have been through, the disappointments, setbacks, injustice. I want to encourage you that there is still something more for you to achieve and that you are above all limits. You may have been pushed down by family members or people around you for a time, but you will arise above your limitations.

'Rejoice not against me, O mine enemy: when I fall, I shall arise; when I sit in darkness, the Lord shall be a light unto me.' **Micah 7:8**

CHAPTER TWO

'Then he which had received the one talent came and said, Lord, I knew thee that thou art an hard man, reaping where thou hast not sown, and gathering where thou hast not strawed: And I was afraid, and went and hid thy talent in the earth: lo, there thou hast that is thine. His Lord answered and said unto him, Thou wicked and slothful servant, thou knewest that I reap where I sowed not, and gather where I have not strawed: Thou oughtest therefore to have put my money to the exchangers, and then at my coming I should have received mine own with usury. Take therefore the talent from him, and give it unto him which hath ten talents' – **Matthew 25:25-28**

Every human being born on this earth has a talent. It does not really matter how small that talent looks, it is still a talent that God has given you. But the question is how many of us have actually discovered that talent within us? We saw in Matthew chapter 25:15, that the master had discovered each person's strength, gift, capability and the ability in each of the servants; he then gave those responsibilities, duties, role or talents matching their ability and went straightway to his journey.

He was expecting to come back to hear good news about how each of the servants had used the talent of gifts he gave them. Therefore we can say that we are gifted or talented in one way or the other. The Bible calls it 'ABILITY'. In Acts 11:29, the disciples were given talent and the ability to enable them to

CHAPTER TWO

minister or send relief to the brethren which were in Judea.

Every talent that God has entrusted to you is to edify the body of Christ and to glorify Him, most importantly in the area of gifts and blessings imparted by the Holy Spirit. You need to acknowledge that each and every talent or ability that you have belongs to the Almighty God and therefore we have the responsibility to ensure that you use those talents in accordance with the purpose for which they have been given.

Paul the Apostle in Romans chapter 12 verses 4-8 made it clear that each and every person is the recipient of every gift they have, and therefore coming together in unity to contribute by using those gifts will make a tremendous impact to the body of Christ. However, discovering talent is one thing and using that talent is another thing all together. If you have a gift for singing and never get training to sharpen and develop it means you are not using that gift, and very soon you will lose that beautiful voice. You cannot blame the devil for your losing that talent or gift of singing - only yourself for not identifying the need for developing it. You may have the gift of serving, teaching, encouraging, contributing to the needs of others or leadership, and you are supposed to use it to glorify God.

'To succeed, you need to find something to hold on to, something to motivate you, something to inspire you.' - **Tony Dorsett**

CHAPTER TWO

Your life will always take shape when you use your talent and gift. For example your career, family, ministry and your community are improved when you use your God-given talent. Have you ever thought how powerful your talent or gift is? Have you sat down and asked yourself how an author becomes a bestseller? How about actors and actresses who have established themselves in the limelight? What about those businessmen who are earning millions by doing what they love and what they do best?

You cannot say you are gifted in playing football or running a hundred meters and not go for training so you can compete with the current world record holder, Usain Bolt, for the gold medal. You cannot be a winner that way. You have to discover yourself, discover your talent and be determined to use that talent fully before it will be recognized and appreciated. Then you may experience and imagine the greater opportunities waiting out there for you if you choose to learn to use your talents.

'Whatsoever thy hand findeth to do, do it with thy might; for there is no work, nor device, nor knowledge, nor wisdom, in the grave, whither thou goest.'- **Ecclesiastes 9.1**

Bob Marley once said 'Life is one big road with lots of signs so when you are riding through the ruts, difficult moments, challenges and fears, do not complicate your mind.' This is to say that you need to remain focused and endure hardship like a soldier on the battlefield. Do not bury your thoughts and your useful ideas.

CHAPTER TWO

'The man with a new idea is a crank - until the idea succeeds' **- Mark Twain**

Tell yourself that you are an inventor and your presence on Earth is to create things that will add value to people. Remember that the days of inventing and being productive through the power of your creative mind are not over; many great and successful men and women did not bury their talents but took the attitude of appreciating the small ideas in themselves and adding skills to turn those ideas into inventions.

Rising above the limitations to your destiny can only be possible if you are fully determined and courageous to live and work smartly on your dreams and purposes for your life. Do not bury your talent under irresponsibility. Take responsibility for your destiny and with the help of God you will be all that He has created you to be. He created you in His image and commanded you to take dominion over ever-creeping things. It is never too late to start using your talents.

'The future belongs to those who believe in the beauty of their dreams.' **- Eleanor Roosevelt**

Don't bury it! In your hands you hold the seeds of failure or the potential for greatness. You can only create your desired future by focusing on the stars, even though things happening around might be limiting you. Begin to ignite the fire that is still burning in you and do not bury your talent.

CHAPTER TWO

'Seeth thou a man diligent in his business, he shall stand before kings and shall not stand before mean men' - **Proverbs 22:29**

The talents you have can only bring light to mankind. Jesus Christ commanded us in Matthew 5: 14 – 16 to be 'the light of the world'. What He was saying here is that our lives and talents should bring clarity to the world. Using your talent will demonstrate to the world how wonderful and creative your God is. The world will be under your feet when you use the talents God has created you with and do not bury it; it will bring light and dispel darkness and ignorance from people's lives and bring salvation to the dying world.

Irrespective of your size, every little gift or talent counts before God - just as a big petrol tanker carrying petrol to the deport needs a certain amount of petrol to get to its destination.

The Lord is counting on you to start using your talents and gifts in singing, teaching the word, praying for the salvation of the soul, nursing and caring for the sick and feeding the poor to bring restoration and revival. Don't be like the unwise servant who went and buried his talent in fear. You are here to take over, not to take cover. No matter how small you think your talent is, just develop it and start using it to the glory of God. By so doing you will not be limited in your endeavours, but God will make you a ruler over many things in Jesus' Name.

CHAPTER THREE

LEARNING NOT TO PUT THINGS OFF

'Go to the ant, you sluggard'; consider its ways and be wise!' - **Proverbs 6:6**

In pursuit of your destiny, you have the responsibility to ensure that everything you do drives you to that desired future. It is your duty to embrace time and let it be your best friend in your journey to your destiny.

'No more limits to your destiny' can only be a reality when you acknowledge the power in your hands to change the way you approach things regarding your future. One thing I have personally learnt over the years is not to have the attitude of procrastination – putting things off.

Developing the right attitude is everything you need to be able to overcome the limitations of life. Zig Ziglar once said that *'others can stop you temporarily, but you are the one who can stop yourself permanently'*. This means that situations will try to limit your progress in life, but develop the right attitude of not giving up in the midst of it all; then you can overcome those limits and get to your destiny in Jesus' Name.

CHAPTER THREE

'To everything there is a season, and a time to every purpose under the heaven' - **Ecclesiastes 3:1**

There is time for everything we do, and it is to your detriment that you waste time because time does not wait for anyone. Therefore in this chapter, we are going to explore some of the reasons why we procrastinate and put limits on our progress in life. We also see some of the best possible ways of overcoming this killer of time.

Procrastination simply means to put off, lay off or postpone an important act or event that should be done in a particular time. This is one of the areas that affect many of us time after time.

In fact what differentiates a successful person from a failure is that successful individuals have the ability to recognize what, when, where, why and how to do something to add value to people around them. A failure on the other hand may not even acknowledge that time is ticking off, but leave everything to time and chance.

Whatever and wherever you may want to get, you have the power to get there through the grace of God, available to all mankind. Until you begin to take some action to fight any form of procrastination, this habit will only steal your opportunities, damage your career and pride or destroy your relationships and ministries.

'Procrastination is the thief of time' - **Edward Young**

CHAPTER THREE

The word of God made an account in the book of Proverbs chapter 6:1-11; encouraging us to observe and acquire some vital knowledge from the ant – 'Go to the ant, you sluggard; consider its ways and be wise'. The ant has no commander, no overseer or ruler, yet it stores its provisions in summer and gathers its food at harvest.

'How long will you lie there, you sluggard? When will you get up from your sleep? A little sleep, a little slumber, a little folding of the hands to rest—and poverty will come on you like a bandit and scarcity like an armed man.' **Proverbs 6:1-11**

Sluggards are those who always enjoy saying 'I will do it later, give me more time to rest' Each and every one of us faces the temptation to procrastinate, thinking we can do something a bit later on and forget that the next thing to come to us is laziness.

The way things are going in the world today and the pressure to meet all demands may pose problems, especially family lives, college works, business meetings to attend, and others are likely to drive you into the habit of procrastination. You may be giving excuses like 'I am waiting for the right time' or 'I am not in the right mood'. These are signs of procrastination which you need to check and avoid.

Many people have their own reasons for procrastination, so you need to examine yourself to see what makes you feel lazy when it is time to do something very important. These

CHAPTER THREE

habits can be in the form of lack of clear goals, underestimating the difficulty of tasks and not being aware of the time required to complete them. One of the main reasons people tend to procrastinate is that they do not have a clear understanding of a particular task, and sometimes think it has been imposed on them by somebody. Often the fear of failure or of success is the reason people are limited in getting to their desired destiny.

In his book 'How to defeat procrastination', Steven Cutler explained that procrastination is a behavioural problem which most of the time, people suffer without realizing that it is already 'eating them alive'. Procrastination can make you unproductive, stressed and guilty about the things you failed to do. More importantly, it can cause people around you to dismiss you as uncooperative and obstructive to the group's progress. This now affects your social relations.

It is a sad fact that many of us have the tendency to procrastinate. Even though it is something that is regarded as unhelpful or even harmful, it may be very hard to find the strength within not to yield to its temptation. However, keep in mind that overcoming procrastination is possible. It can be easy and is highly recommendable to cast out procrastination from your system if you are serious in getting to your destiny.

'You may delay, but time will not' - **Benjamin Franklin**

CHAPTER THREE

Ladders to climb to overcome procrastination

There are many ways to overcome the habit of procrastination in order to get to your destiny. It takes the spirit of concentration and commitment to do this. Do not waste time you could have used in building wealth, happiness and life contentment to add value to your generation.

The following are some ladders to climb to overcome procrastination. Ladders are used typically for reaching heights. When you are not tall enough, the ladder is strategically placed to ensure safety. Therefore in order to overcome and climb over your limitations, you need the ladders to empower you to get your height of destiny. These are the ladders:

1. MOTIVATE YOURSELF

We read in proverbs 6:7 that the ants have no leaders or instructors to push them into greatness. That is, they have to motivate themselves ('It has no commander, overseer, or ruler'). What is motivating you in life? What is your motivation in studying, working or serving God? Are you doing it because you think you have to do it? Do you do what you do because someone told you to? Are you serving God because you are expecting a miracle from Him, or going to church because you do not want your church leaders to be calling you and asking you questions - so you go to church to warm the benches?

What is driving you to do what you are doing in the first place? Let your motivation come from inside you as you read the word of God and not from the outside, to please men. My brethren, it doesn't depend on your situation, feelings or who you are working with or for. You may not be appreciated for what you may be doing in your employment, school, university, church, house or among the family, but you need to motivate yourself to keep the faith and press on to the prize awaiting for you. Your salary may have been delayed by your boss, but as you are motivated to work hard and smartly, you will begin to see that you are progressing in life because what the enemy meant for evil, God will turn to your favour.

It is interesting to know that the ants do not need anybody to motivate them. They do not need a Prime Minister or NATO, neither do they need United Nations to motivate them. Who are you waiting to motivate you? Let the word of God motivate you in all you do.

The Bible tells of David's return from the land of the Philistines with his 600-man army to the village of Ziklag. Upon arrival they saw that the Amalekites had invaded, burning their houses to the ground and kidnapping their wives and children. This horrible news caused David's small army to turn on him and talk of stoning him to death. With no one to turn to for advice, David could just accept his fate. One thing we know is that David was greatly distressed; for the people spoke of stoning him, because the soul of all the people was grieved, every man for his sons and for his daughters: but David encouraged (motivated) himself in the LORD his God.

'Whatever you are doing, work at it with enthusiasm, as to the Lord and not for people' - **Colossians 3:23**

2. PLAN AHEAD

Planning ahead is one of the ladders you need to overcome procrastination. It can help organize your day and your busy schedule. To be able to be all that the Lord has called you to be and get to your destiny, planning ahead is a great way to prioritize and schedule those events and activities in a strategic manner.

No matter how busy your life, work, family and children make you, you still need to plan ahead. Don't wait until the last minute. Maybe you see others procrastinating until the last minute, and it makes you worry that things will never get done in time. Regardless of which of these profiles suits you, planning helps everyone work together while still getting everything done in a team.

From the passage we read in proverbs 6:1-11, we discovered that the ants always plan ahead. We learned that they gather their food in preparation for the winter. They work hard during the summer when food supplies are abundant and enjoy them during the winter, when supplies are scarce.

Do you know when your 'summer' and your 'winter' season are, to gather the things you may be needing when the time arises? Do you know when to work or study hard and when you need to rest? Have you planned for the future? Have you done your best in whatever you are doing at the moment? Are you studying hard to get a job in the future, to work hard for your savings, to serve God wholeheartedly for your 'heavenly investment?'

Did you know that effective planning saves hours of headache and worries? Planning ahead helps you overcome hours of confusion and gives you enough energy to tackle tasks, helping you to maximize your full potential to step into your desired future. Anybody who is addicted to planning is able to maintain focus on specific objectives and direct resources on the most important things in creating their sure future.

Know that whatever you do now will not be in vain, no matter how silly or irrelevant it may seem to you. Maybe you are working part time in a restaurant, or maybe you are studying something that you think is unrelated to your course - whatever it may be, God can always make something good come out of it. You'll learn something that you would never have thought before, without realizing it! Whatever it is, plan ahead.

3. BE DECISIVE

Every great leap forward in your life comes after you have made a clear decision of some kind. Decisiveness is about making a decision or a choice. A person who is decisive is able to make a clear distinction between options. In Deuteronomy 30:19, we read that God spoke through Moses to the children of Israel regarding their choice of decision: *'I call heaven and earth to record this day against you, that I have set before you life and death, blessing and cursing: therefore choose life, that both thou and thy seed may live.'*

Again in Joshua 1:8, we saw that Joshua was instructed to make the choice to meditate on the word of God for his success. *'This book of the law shall not depart out of thy mouth; but thou shalt meditate therein day and night, that thou mayest observe to do according to all that is written therein: for then thou shalt make thy way prosperous, and then thou shalt have good success.'*

Joshua 24:15 *'And if it seem evil unto you to serve the LORD, choose you this day whom ye will serve; whether the gods which your fathers served that were on the other side of the flood, or the gods of the Amorites, in whose land ye dwell: but as for me and my house, we will serve the LORD.'*

The ants made a decision to prepare and gather food at the right time. They searched for and discovered the right moment for them to get out of their nests and hiding places to search for what was needful and important to their destiny.

CHAPTER THREE

They were not too lazy to get out from their so-called comfort zone. I am very sure that they were faced with fire and dangerous events which could have limited them from chasing their sure future. They were not hindered by the rocks, blocks, lizards, snakes and other things that could have posed a threat to them. The ants were fully determined to attain their destiny.

'No power in the sky above or in the earth below - indeed, nothing in all creation - will ever be able to separate us from the love of God that is revealed in Christ Jesus our Lord' - **Romans 8:39**

Are you always in your comfort zone, too lazy or too scared to go out because your mind tells you that there is a lion in the street or snow on the road? In Proverbs 22:13; the sluggard says, *'There is a lion outside! I shall be killed in the streets!'* My brothers and sister in the Lord; do not be too scared to try something that you have not done before. Take the step of faith and get into that field and take the initiative like the ants. Each and every creature created by God is likely to face challenges, but we are admonished by the word of God not to be dismayed or discouraged.

I have also discovered that ants are the most delicate because of their sizes and, are prone to fatality as they are too small to notice. Therefore they can be trampled upon, but they are not scared to take chances to come out of their nests to achieve their goals and purpose.

CHAPTER THREE

'And there were four leprous men at the entrance of the gate: and they said one to another, why sit we here until we die?' - **2 kings 7:3**

These were individuals who made a strong decision to get up to pursue their destiny and not allow their leprosy to hinder or limit them. They were fully determined that whatever their situation, they would go and get something. In those days any person with such an infectious disease had to wear torn clothes, let his hair be unkempt, cover the lower part of his face and cry out, 'Unclean! Unclean!' They did not allow public ridicule to stop them - they believed in the power of decisiveness.

The choice you make on a daily basis affects what you will have, be or do in the tomorrows of your life.

It is very important that you do not postpone decisions you need to make today for your family, children, job, marriage, relationship and your future, because it could have dire consequences for the future. Be decisive!

4. FOCUS ON YOUR ASSIGNMENT

Life is a journey which must be travelled with focus. You cannot get to your destination safely without focusing on the road to success. You cannot get to the mountain top without focus. The higher you climb the mountain of success, the more you need to train your mind to focus. A pilot or a driver

CHAPTER THREE

cannot get his passengers to where he is going safely without remaining focused.

In my field of work, you cannot be a surgeon or a nurse undertaking the responsibility of caring for patients unless you focus on the particular patient allocated to you in the intensive care unit. This makes it clear that we all need the spirit of focus to enable us to overcome any limitations that may face us.

On the road to your destiny, you need to understand that there may be some obstacles and challenges. Jesus Christ and His disciples were faced with a severe storm (Mark 6:45-56), but they survived. This means that with the power of focus, you can achieve your dream. You only get to your destination or your future when you are willing to remain steadfast and focused. I have decoded the word FOCUS into two statements which really make sense.
Face Odd Circumstances Until you Succeed
Or:
Fight Obstacles Continuously Until you Succeed.

When you want to be a high achiever, you need to fight continuously until you succeed in life. When examining the movement of an ant, we see that they all move in one direction irrespective of distraction.

Focusing on an assignment is very important in overcoming the habit of procrastination. We can observe that all ants focus on one thing, such as preparing and gathering food for the winter season. Are you equally focused on your God-given assignment? Remain focused and do not look at what is happening around you to distract you from getting to your destiny. You must search through yourself to see what threatens to take your focus away from your assignment.

Be like the ants and do not give up easily. Successful people are never satisfied with their current level of achievement, neither are they limited by any form of disability. No matter what terrain they are going through, the ants keep on carrying the food without ever giving up. The Lord is on their side and yours.

'*Success is a result of good decision making - failure is a result of bad decision making*'- **Bishop Michael Hutton-Wood**

5. DEVELOP A SPIRIT OF SELF-DISCIPLINE

I heard Bishop Michael Hutton-Wood once say that 'self discipline is the ability to make yourself do what you should do, when you should do it, whether you feel like it or not'. Developing a spirit of self-discipline is actually mastering your self-confidence, self-esteem and inner strength, to produce self satisfaction. It is sometimes said that people with lack of self-discipline often become failures. In view of this, it is possible to say that self-discipline is one of the ladders that will enable you to remain focused on your destiny.

CHAPTER THREE

When you look at the way an automobile works, it relies on its parts to be reliable. For example, you need the gearbox, clutch, brakes, wheels, headlights, hazard lights, just to mention a few to enable it to function. So it is also vital that you have self-discipline as a vital part in your life to be able to overcome any limitations before you. Self-discipline should be the fuel in your petrol tank to get you to your destiny.

This life is full challenges, and sometimes a challenge tends to distract your focus and purpose for a particular day. However, when you are disciplined enough to remain on track you will surely get to that place of fulfillment. Imagine travelling on a highway and coming across a number of lights indicating that you should reduce your speed. You do not change your mind about the journey but discipline yourself to continue it. The journey into your destiny will be limited by so many roadworks, traffic lights and sometimes other drivers pulling in front or across you, so it will take discipline to remain the driver you were when you first began the journey without getting upset and angry.

In my field of work I have seen this demonstrated when an individual decides to quit smoking or other health-related problem like drinking and drug addiction. It takes self-discipline to overcome them. Do not allow the flood of procrastination to creep into your life or take you by surprise. Use these ladders to overcome the tsunami of procrastination. You can do it.

CHAPTER THREE

'Discipline is the power that fuels the systems that LEAD you to larger goals.' **(unknown)**

6. LET THE WORD OF GOD DWELL IN YOU

'Let the word of Christ dwell in you richly in all wisdom; teaching and admonishing one another in psalms and hymns and spiritual songs, singing with grace in your hearts to the Lord.' Colossians 3:16 and Romans 15:4 inform us that for everything that was written in the past was written to teach us, so that through endurance and the encouragement of the scriptures we might have hope. Make yourself get into the word of God. Even if it seems dry and lifeless to you, keep reading and you will be encouraged and uplifted.

When we allow God's Word to dwell in our lives, it changes and transforms us unto the image of God himself. It also becomes treasured in our lives. *'All Scripture is given by inspiration of God, and is profitable for doctrine, for reproof, for correction, for instruction in righteousness, that the man of God may be complete, thoroughly equipped for every good work.'* - **Timothy 3:16**

Furthermore, the word of God allows us to shed negative things that disturbed us at one time, and in many cases, overcame us. Amazingly, the word of God makes you healthy in your physical appearance, with the glory of the Lord shining in your face. Meditating on God's word creates

CHAPTER THREE

calmness in your inner spirit and even eliminates or reduces the symptoms of many illnesses.

'Do not let this Book of the Law depart from your mouth; meditate on it day and night, so that you may be careful to do everything written in it. Then you will be prosperous and successful' **- Joshua 1:8 (New International Version)**

CHAPTER FOUR

STAYING AWAY FROM TOXIC RELATIONSHIPS

Building great relationships takes time and energy. Many people only discover how valuable such relationships are when they are tested. One author writes: 'Contouring your heart to beat with another requires extensive whittling, to trim away self-centredness. Some says that it's like riding the bus; if you are going to have company you must then be willing to stop over to accommodate other people and their baggage they bring.'

Any individual in your life influencing you negatively (ungodly counsels) should never be allowed to remain as a friend. In 2 Samuel 13:1-29, we were told how an individual person's kingship was destroyed just because of toxic friendship. Jonadab was Amnon's best friend and they had lived together for years, possibly sharing ideas, dreams, vision, and goals. A time came when Jonadab needed an advice from his so-called friend Amnon regarding his future. That one piece of advice actually cost his future as king.

'*And it came to pass after this, that Absalom the son of David*

CHAPTER FOUR

had a fair sister, whose name was Tamar; and Amnon the son of David loved her. And Amnon was so vexed, that he fell sick for his sister Tamar; for she was a virgin; and Amnon thought it hard for him to do anything to her. But Amnon had a friend, whose name was Jonadab, the son of Shimeah David's brother: and Jonadab was a very subtil man. And he said unto him, Why art thou, being the king's son, lean from day to day? wilt thou not tell me? And Amnon said unto him, I love Tamar, my brother Absalom's sister. And Jonadab said unto him, Lay thee down on thy bed, and make thyself sick: and when thy father cometh to see thee, say unto him, I pray thee, let my sister Tamar come, and give me meat, and dress the meat in my sight, that I may see it, and eat it at her hand.

'So Amnon lay down, and made himself sick: and when the king was come to see him, Amnon said unto the king, I pray thee, let Tamar my sister come, and make me a couple of cakes in my sight, that I may eat at her hand. Then David sent home to Tamar, saying, Go now to thy brother Amnon's house, and dress him meat. So Tamar went to her brother Amnon's house; and he was laid down. And she took flour, and kneaded it, and made cakes in his sight, and did bake the cakes. And she took a pan, and poured them out before him; but he refused to eat. And Amnon said, Have out all men from me. And they went out every man from him. And Amnon said unto Tamar, Bring the meat into the chamber that I may eat of thine hand. And Tamar took the cakes *which she had made, and brought them into the chamber to Amnon her brother. And when she had brought them unto him to eat, he took hold of her, and said unto her, come lie with me, my sister...* ' The story continued.

This is the main reason why you need to be careful about those you allow into your life as friends. Any friendship that does not add to you, increase, appreciate, establish or multiply you, but subtracts, makes life worse or brings you failure should be cut off. It does not matter how long the friendship has lasted. You are safer breaking that friendship before your life is broken down alongside your health. Be open and frank with such 'toxic friends' and let them know that you cannot get anywhere with their negative influences on your life. Remember that such toxic friendships are like a car with flat tyres. You cannot go anywhere until you change those tyres.

Friendship is a choice you make and not legally demanded.

Who is the friend in your life that you share your dreams and ideas with? Whoever he or she is, you need to be very careful because it could really cost your destiny. In proverbs 18:24, Solomon said *'there is a friend who sticks closer than a brother'*. Relationship is about quality, not quantity. That is why heart connection can be so much stronger than blood connections when it comes to relationships. *'Can two walk together, except they be agreed?'* - **Amos 3:3 KJV.**

Any friendship void of agreement is 100% subject to lack of achievement in life.

CHAPTER FOUR

Staying away from toxic relationships or friendships means that you have the responsibility to avoid relationships that may have a negative influence on your life and hinder you from getting to your destiny. When it comes between your purposes in life you need to actually search for those people who may discourage you from your assignment in life and avoid them completely.

It is very important to know that people you call friends are very necessary in achieving your purpose in life. They are either adding to you or subtracting from you. They are either making your life better or making it worse. You decide the types of friendship you want to keep or to avoid in order to get to your sure destiny.

'*A righteous person is cautious with friendship, but the way of the wicked leads them astray*' - **Proverbs 12:26**

To be able to overcome the limitations to destiny, it is crucial to take your time and assess the types of friendship you have in your life. If there are friendships or relationships that regularly affect your productivities emotionally and sometimes affect your health, it is about time you decided to keep them or get rid of them completely so as to get to your sure future.

'*People in our lives are like buttons in an elevator which take us up to the top floor, keep us on the ground or to the basement.*'
- **Bishop Michael Hutton-Wood**

In Psalms 1:1, we are admonished not to even walk with

CHAPTER FOUR

them: *'Blessed is the man that walketh not in the counsel of the ungodly, nor standeth in the way of sinners, nor sitteth in the seat of the scornful'*.

You must avoid the company of those people who do not in any way share your vision or have your interest at heart. You must do everything to protect and preserve your destiny. God has a purpose, a plan for you, and a brighter and greater future. This is why you must not allow negative people to sow seeds of discouragement in your life and distract you from God's divine purpose for you.

It is not easy to stay away from so-called friends, but my fellow believers, it will be in your best interests to do whatever you can do to stay away from them. A negative individual or friend has the tendency to influence your character and behaviours. Birds of a feather flock together.

Interestingly, you cannot determine the outcome of a relationship and know if that person in your life will continue to remain the dependable and reliable individual they were when you first met them. More often than not, it is not very easy to identify any destructive friendship, but it is good to be aware of this possibility.

As you decide to overcome the things that hinder you from reaching your goals in life, it is also vital to be aware of those friends that set themselves as negative critics in your life. These individuals could be limiting you by reminding you of your past mistakes and shortfalls.

CHAPTER FOUR

'Now I beseech you, brethren, mark them which cause divisions and offences contrary to the doctrine which ye have learned; and avoid them. For they that are such serve not our Lord Jesus Christ, but their own belly; and by good words and fair speeches deceive the hearts of the simple.' - **Romans 16:17-18**

It is important that you treat people the same way you would like them to treat you. You need to see and assess the benefits of your friends in your life. Each and every one of us needs friends in our lives. No one is an island. We need friends who will help us get to our destiny and are willing to accommodate us during the good and the bad times.

Therefore these are the types of relationship or friendship that you need in your life. You need a friend who will enable you and empower you to make good decisions regarding crucial moments in your life. Wouldn't you want a good friend to lift you up when you have fallen into the gutter?

'Iron sharpeneth iron; so a man sharpeneth the countenance of his friend.' - **Proverbs 27:17 King James Bible (Cambridge Ed.)**

When it comes to your achievement in life, there will be different kinds of individual who will be attracted to you. These people can be classified as pilot friends, first-class friends and economy friends determining your flight in life.

CHAPTER FOUR

PILOT FRIENDSHIPS

These kinds of individuals are friends in your life serving as mentors and giving you speed in whatever you do. They board your friendship flight to motivate you, encourage and sometimes takes the ultimate responsibility to ensure that you achieve your dream. A pilot friend adds value to you and propels you to get to that sure goal that you have set for yourself. They share your vision and sometimes will go all the way to stay with you until you become all that God has made you to be. They never leave you along the way, regardless of your mistakes. They actually see great treasure in you and bring the gold out of you.

Remember that this kind of individual in your life does not spy on you but is always there to celebrate your success. They are very concerned about your failures, because they can see the greatness in your life and will go all the way to encourage you to get to the top. Pilot friends know your weaknesses, but will not remind or dwell on a negative past or limit your progress in the pursuit of your dreams. They will rather show your strengths even in the midst of fearful events, just to fortify your faith, free your spirit whenever there is anxiety. They do not leave you in mid air. They become your pillar in life.

FIRST CLASS FRIENDSHIPS

These types of friends also gravitate toward you, simply

because you share the same vision with them. They only stay with you as long as they can get something from you. Sometimes when situations get worst and things are not getting the way they think they should be they get offended and give all kinds of excuse to stay away from you, even though they share the same vision with you. They have different agendas regarding the fulfillment of their dreams and will only give you limited information as to what to do to achieve God's purpose for your life.

ECONOMY FRIENDSHIPS

Economy friends are those who come into your life only because of what you can give them. They do not add value to you but are always there to collect and receive from you. Although they also share your vision, they will not be happy if you are doing better than them. They will do everything possible to keep you in economy class with them. They are only happy for you until you decide to do something productive with your life. They will say things like 'We are all managing fine here and now you are saying that you have to move on in life'. They will frustrate you from moving higher.

Even though you are thinking positive to remain focused on your assignment in life, these individuals will have negative ideas about you. You need to keep a positive attitude even when you are in the midst of these toxic friends. Develop and establish defence mechanisms or boundaries to create your own happiness when you are around them.

Toxic friends do not only limit themselves - they also limit the progress of people around them. They also cease to add value or contribution to the friendship that you have with them and cause division among you and more productive friends who are willing to come into your life. Stay away from them!

Life is not built on selfishness and self-centredness; it's built on productive and relevant relationships.

CHAPTER FIVE

STANDING FIRM ON YOUR PURPOSE IN LIFE

'Above all, you must live as citizens of heaven, conducting yourselves in a manner worthy of the Good News about Christ. Then, whether I come and see you again or only hear about you, I will know that you are standing together with one spirit and one purpose, fighting together for the faith, which is the Good News.'
- Philippians 1:27, New Living Translation (©2007)

Getting to your destiny involves a journey. It is therefore possible to say that life is a journey and you must embark on every life journey with a definite purpose. Living a life without a definite purpose is living without bearings. For you to be able to overcome limitations against your destiny, you need to have, and live by, a purpose.

Standing firm on your purpose in life means being steadfast, solid, unmovable and unshakable in that which you have set before you to achieve in life (GOALS). It means being fully persuaded that no matter what happens you will stand firm on that purpose that the Lord God has placed in your heart.

CHAPTER FIVE

Everything on earth is created by God and has a purpose attached to its existence. You were created for God's divine purpose, and that is to live to glorify Him by living purposefully and not aimlessly. You are not here on earth just to eat and die but to add value to mankind. You are unique simply because of your purpose on this planet. Nobody looks like you and nobody has the same purpose as you, just as every car engine is made to fit a particular car model. You are created to answer to a specific question on Earth.

'Before I formed you in the womb I knew you, before you were born I set you apart. I appointed you as a prophet to the nations' **- Jeremiah 1:5**

When you look around you, you will appreciate the purpose of telephones, computers, radios, fax machines and many more. These gadgets are serving the purpose for which they were created. Have you identified the purpose for which you were created?

You may be asking yourself, what is my purpose in life? Why am I here?

The purpose of a mango seed is to continue the multiplication of mangoes in the world. The word of God says that everything has a purpose under the sun; a time and a season.

'A time to be born, and a time to die; a time to plant, and a time to pluck up that which is planted' **- Ecclesiastes 3:2**

Almighty God has always wanted to have a relationship

CHAPTER FIVE

with you. He wants a family relationship, as He is our father. This is the main reason why He sent His son Jesus Christ to come on Earth to die on the cross to save us from our sinful natures. Jesus Christ did not come on earth to be a politician, a lawyer, taxi driver or a carpenter, even though his father was a carpenter by trade. He came to live his purpose as a saviour of souls and to be a bridge to cross back to the Heavenly Father (God).

God has a purpose and a plan for our lives. We learn from Hebrews 10:7 that we are created for a specific purpose and as we identify that purpose and plan for our lives, we will begin to have a meaningful and successful life.

However, there is a need to sit ourselves down and undertake careful assessments of our needs and count the cost involved in our dreams. Having a purpose alone is not enough. You need to count the cost of what it may take to realize the dream (purpose) and hold fast on to it.

'Daniel purposed in his heart that he would not defile himself with the portion of the king's meat nor with the wine which he drank, therefore he requested the prince of the eunuchs that he might not defile himself' - **Daniel 1:8**

Standing firm on your purpose enables you to withstand and bear almost everything. This also makes your life very simple, as you become more definite on what exactly you want to achieve in life and when. You do not leave your life anyhow but with a sure purpose.

CHAPTER FIVE

A meaningless life erodes the cells of your life and is worse than cancer cells.

Standing firm on your purpose demands that you keep your eyes fixed exclusively on your dream or goal. You will need absolute focus, disregarding any distractions, wherever they may be coming from. You will require extreme devotion, commitment and the determination to realize the dream or goal at all cost.

Can you imagine what can happen when a footballer who has placed the ball at the spot and is waiting for the referee to whistle for him/her to take a penalty decides to look aside as he kicks? Or the driver who fixes his/her attention on the sandwich box by his side, rather than concentrating on the road?

A purposeful person is one who defies all odds and stands by the truth. He may buy the truth, but will not sell it. He/she is that individual who makes up his/her mindset with its focus without allowing any wind of change to distract them.

The ability to succeed in any endeavour of life and develop the capacity to have a positive impact on others is dependent on self-denials, sacrifices and commitments as evidenced in what we have already read about in the book of Daniel above.

'Purpose is the power that pushes you forward in reaching God's destiny for your life.' - **Olga Hermans**

Clearly Daniel's purpose was not to defile himself with the king's meat, as he knew what the consequences could be. He

CHAPTER FIVE

no doubt denied himself so as to conform to Babylonian custom. The journey could be rugged, the tree full of thorns, disappointments and varieties of challenges, but you must not despair and lose the plot. Rather must you hold firm and strong with a great faith like that of the proverbial mustard seed and remain focused on your dream, your goal, and soon victory will be in sight in God's own time.

As we read in **2 Corinthians 4:18** *'While we look not at the things which are seen but at the things which are not seen, for the things which are seen are temporal, but the things which are not seen are eternal'*.

When you are not moved or perturbed by the distractions, challenges and discouragements of loved ones and the devil's tricks in aborting your dream by taking your eyes off your target, in no time you will appreciate that these holdups are nothing compared to the fulfillment of a dream come through.

As you make up your mind to be in fellowship with our Heavenly Father, accepting his beloved son Jesus as our personal saviour, who died on the cross that we may be saved, holding on to his promises through his word, nothing - and I mean nothing - should separate you from this relationship.

'I will stand upon my watch and set me upon the tower, and will watch to see what he will say unto me, and what I shall answer when I am reproved. And the Lord answered me, and said, write the vision and make it plain upon tables that he may run that

CHAPTER FIVE

readeth it. For the vision is yet for an appointed time, but at the end it shall speak and not lie, though it tarry, wait for it, because it will surely come, it will not tarry.' - **Habakkuk 2: 1-3**

'Life without a purpose is life without meaning and the greatest tragedy in life is not death, but life without purpose' - **Dr. Myles Munroe**

The book of Genesis records the story of Joseph. Genesis 37:5 says, 'One night Joseph had a dream'. Joseph's family was like many other people today. They didn't understand or appreciate his dream. In fact, it was because of his dream that his brothers sold him into slavery. And Joseph went though many difficult years when it seemed as if his dream would never come to pass.

God had a very special plan for Joseph's life, which was shown to him through dreams. The Lord also has a perfect plan for your life; He may not reveal it to you through a dream that comes while you are asleep, but He will give you the desire to bring that plan into fulfilment.

When you became a born-again believer, something very special happened to you: you received your birthright as a joint-heir of God with Jesus Christ. You now belong to the Father in Heaven. People with spiritual birthrights are called by the Lord to fulfill His plan on earth, and that is why the Lord gives them spiritual dreams. It is His way of causing them to 'occupy' and be fruitful until the return of Jesus.

CHAPTER FIVE

Has the Lord given you a dream or purpose? That is a spiritual dream; you don't have to receive the Lord's call through a vision which comes in your sleep! Your inner desire to bring a specific plan into fulfilment is your dream. If you don't have a specific goal, get one! Without a purpose (vision, dream) you will drift aimlessly along life's flow. With a dream you will be fruitful and fulfilled in whatever you do.

God gave Joseph a spiritual dream, and his brothers hated him. When Joseph told his brothers about the dream, and shared it with his father, Jacob became upset. At first he didn't understand how Joseph could imagine such things, but then Jacob began considering the contents of Joseph's dream, and he began to believe that there was something more to it than he had initially realized.

Jacob discerned Joseph's dream with spiritual judgment, but his sons did not discern it at all; in fact they were plotting against Joseph. They thought he was a dreamer. Doesn't that sound like what the world has to say about Christians? They sometimes say, 'Oh, those Christians are such dreamers! They should stop all that dreaming and get back to reality.'

Be prepared for the reaction of people around you, for they will often misunderstand you. Some people might even think you're crazy. So what? You have a dream, a goal which they might not have. Just like Joseph's brothers, they had no understanding of spiritual dreams, and when Joseph approached them they banded together and grabbed him, stripping him of his colourful coat. They hated that coat with a passion.

Right then, Joseph's life took an unconventional path. After being sold into slavery, he was thrown into prison, accused of things he had not done. But later Joseph realized that these difficult times helped prepare him to fulfil his dream.

Joseph eventually was elevated to second-in-command of Egypt. After his father died, and his brothers stood before him, he said to them, 'You intended to harm me, but God intended it all for good. He brought me in this position so I could save the lives of many people.' Gen.50:20 NLT

According to Olga Hermans, 'Many people have dreams, but they don't make any preparations to accomplish them'. They think that if their dream is from God, it will just happen. But those who have accomplished the desires burning in their hearts can tell you that it didn't 'just' happen. There was some hard work involved. Preparation time can be difficult. But without it, you can't step into your DESTINY. Preparation is never easy, but when the time comes to step into your DESTINY, you're ready. When Joseph's time came, he acted on his dream (Gen 41:14).

Joseph didn't sit in prison wondering, 'Should I do this or not?' You may think that sounds crazy, but many people today sit in the prison of their thoughts, refusing to act on

CHAPTER FIVE

opportunities knocking at their door. Joseph acted on the opportunity presented to him and stepped into his DESTINY.

Are you ready to step up to the plate and accomplish what God placed on the inside of you? I encourage you to endure whatever hardship you are experiencing. Know that it will pay off in the end. And when you finally step up to the plate of your DESTINY, it will outshine the endurance that it took to get there. That's why people call the past 'the good old days.' The process may not seem like a good place to be at all. But when their dream, their destiny became a reality, all of that hardship didn't mean anything anymore.

No matter what you are facing, don't give up on your dream. It's worth standing for. It's worth fighting for. It's worth enduring the difficulties for until it becomes a reality.

When you have a dream, don't let the enemy steal it. Joseph had to wait thirteen years before it came to pass. Stand firm and hold on to your purpose. Remember there will always be obstacles to limits which can throw you off your destiny. These obstacles are a way to make a stronger you. They are there for you to use and control.

Everything in your life is something you can control. That is the number one thing you must never forget. You can achieve what you want to achieve if you believe you can.

No more limits to your destiny.

CHAPTER SIX

THE POWER OF PRAYER IN YOUR LIFE

Isaiah 52:1, Eph 6:12, Dan 32:11, I Sam.30:1-8, Deut 20:24, Dan1:2

'For we (you) wrestle not against flesh and blood, but against principalities, against power of rulers of darkness of this world, against spiritual wickedness in high places.' - **Ephesians 6:12**

God has a master plan for you for the rest of your life. He said in Jeremiah 1:5 that before you were formed, He knew you. This is to say that nobody is useless in the world. God so loved the world that he gave His Son to come and die on the cross to restore us back to the original purpose to serve and worship him.

God created us to serve Him. He created you for a specific purpose and made you to shine wherever you go. Nothing in the world that happens to you surprises God (Romans 9:10-15).

He created all things and knows all things. He separated you for his glory not to shame you. Your future is not in your plan but in God's plan for you. Therefore until you discover that plan, purpose, vision and goal He has for you, you cannot live to glorify Him and you will live a frustrated life.

CHAPTER SIX

However, after you have discovered your purpose in life and are doing everything to achieve that dream or purpose, the enemy will not sit down to drink hot chocolate because you have identified that purpose for your life. He will attack you from all angles just to derail or abort that vision.

The enemies of progress will set in to frustrate your hard work and your perseverance to your assignment. *'And they came to the chief priests and elders, and said , We have bound ourselves under a great curse, that we will eat nothing until we have slain Paul'* - **Acts 23:14**

The devil knows how powerful you will be when you actually discover and implement your purpose, and that is the main reason why he tries to attack your dream or vision. There is no promised land that you need to get to that is without a battle. All battles in life are as a result of one vision or the other.

'Life is not a funfair but a war-fare' - **Dr Michael Hutton - Wood.**

Anytime a vision or a dream is shown to an individual, the devil strikes to get that dream aborted. The dream, vision, purpose and seed you carry will always attract the enemy's attack. We saw in the lives of Moses, Joseph, Paul and our Lord Jesus Christ, just to mention a few, how the enemy did that what he could to destroy or kill God's purpose over their lives. You are not exempted.

CHAPTER SIX

The devil will do everything to attack your dream. The word of God says that 'you are the head and not the tail', and in view of that the enemy will do everything to get you to the tail instead of you being the head.

Your purpose in life is not to attract butterflies but bees.

The good news is that God has given us the Power of Prayer, which we can engage any time and anywhere to destroy the works of the enemies who try to limit us. One thing the devil fears is a prayerful person, because prayer is the weapon in the life of a believer.

Living above your limitations and getting to your destiny can only be possible if you engage in prayer. Prayer breaks the shackles of the enemies and sets us free from the attacks of destiny destroyers. Prayer is the act of pleading fervently or asking and seeking God for something with intense yearning.

'Pray without ceasing' - **1 Thessalonians 5:17**

God wants to birth his purpose and vision through you and only through prayer (intimacy with God) that He can use you. Many people have never thought it necessary to pray for their destiny. They get up in the morning and rush to the bathroom, get breakfast, get into their car and zoom off without praying or seeking God's face for His leading or direction for the day. They live their life anyhow without prayer.

Some have many excuses for not praying. That is a big mistake. The devil is having a free ride any time you do not

CHAPTER SIX

pray for your destiny or purpose. He comes in and messes your plans, ideas, business, education, marriage, finances and relationship because prayer is missing in your life.

'And from the days of John the Baptist until now the kingdom of heaven suffereth violence, and the violent take it by force' - **Matthew 11:12 KJV**

Let me tell you a story that was told by C. Peter Wagner of an incident that took place on an airliner. For the purpose of this example, all names are changed. I will call the believer KAFUI and the devil's agent MR. SHAME.

On this particular flight, Kafui, who was a Christian and a devoted believer, was sitting next to another handsome man (Mr Shame) in the business class. During the flight, Kafui noticed that Mr Shame had bowed his head and was moving his lips as if he was praying.

When Mr. Shame had finished his so-called praying, Kafui thought he was also a believer and a Christian because of the prayer posture. So Kafui engaged in conversation with him and asked him if he was a pastor or intercessor. Mr Shame replied astonishingly that he was actually an agent of the devil with an assignment to bring about the fall of believers and their families who have identified their purpose in life. He went on to say that he was sent to put limitations before anyone going to achieve success in their business, education, marriage, finances, churches and ministry and to derail them from getting to their sure destiny.

CHAPTER SIX

After a short conversation, Mr Shame went back to his posture to ensure that his main purpose on the plane materialized. In fact the encounter made Kafui realize how crucial and powerful prayer is in the journey of life.

The devil's agenda is to put limits, blockages and pains in your life to stop you from getting or achieving your dream and to get rid of you. You may not actually know the kind of mayhem and bitter experiences that the devil put in your life just to make you quit that dream and purpose.

Dedicate your time and life to pray for your destiny, because the evil ones are not resting and sleeping. They are working overtime to see you fall, derail, die, lose that job, etc.

'Prayer is what it takes to bring heavenly resources to meet the needs on earth.' - **W F Kumuyi (Deeper Life Bible Church)**

It is prayer that put God to work on your behalf. Prayer puts your angel to work fighting your invisible enemies against your destiny.

I have come to realize that prayer actually brings into play heavenly forces to act on my family life, especially in the life of my wife. At one point in our life when she was due to give birth to our son Prince Joshua, the devil attacked her so seriously that she ended up on a life support machine for weeks in Intensive Care Unit (ITU) in the United Kingdom. But when our church began to pray, led by Bishop Michael Hutton-Wood, God heard our prayer and answered. My wife's life was delivered from the spirit of death.

CHAPTER SIX

The devil foresaw the potential in her womb and tried to attack it, simply because my wife was going to give birth to her purpose after nine months of hard work and sleepless nights. The devil is a liar. He has been defeated in Jesus' Name.

The devil will always attack you because of the seed (purpose/dreams/potential) you carry.

Your heavenly father has placed great things in you and it takes prayer to release their potential. Every movement or step you take in life should be backed by prayer. The power of prayer enables you to get closer to God. It gives you direct connection to God to experience divine intimacy with Him.

A time came in Solomon's life when he needed to hear from God concerning the purpose and the direction for his life. He went to God in prayer to enquire of God his plan for him. In 11 Chronicles 7:12-15, we heard: *'And the Lord appeared to Solomon by night and said unto him, I have heard your prayer and have chosen this place myself, for a house of sacrifice...*' When you read on you will see that Solomon offered his sacrifice at the appointed place. Divine instruction and direction is what you get from God when you engage in the power of prayer.

From the following passages, Matthew 7:7-8; John 16:13; Philippians 4:6-7; Ephesians 1:17, 18; you will see that when you engage in the power of prayerful life, you begin to express your thanks, your faith, your love and your hopes with God in prayer. This then makes you receive from Him answers, assurance, guidance, peace, strength and power, revelation of who He is and what He wants to do.

'Prayer fulfils the Purpose of God in Salvation' - **Michael Fackerell**

According to Michael Fackerell, if you desire to see miraculous results in your life you need to engage in effective prayer and fasting. We spend time with God in prayer and communion because we love him. Just as a man and woman in love desire to be together and communicate, so do we if we love God. You will desire to be with Him and in fellowship with Him in proportion to your love for Him.

The power of prayer makes you know that God is your source. He is your life (Colossians 3:4). Through prayer you receive the comfort, the strength and all the other resources that you need in life to make it. Through lack of prayer, you become weak, while others and Satan gain the advantage in your lives.

'Watch and pray, lest you enter into temptation.' - **Mt. 26:41.**
'Continue earnestly in prayer, being vigilant in it with thanksgiving' - **Colossians 4:2.**

Prayer is so vital to all that God wants to do on the Earth, through you, with you and for you. Your purpose on earth is the reason why the devil is fighting you and your family. 'No more limits to your destiny' becomes a reality in your life

CHAPTER SIX

when you start to pray. Remember that you become an agent of God when you engage in prayer daily. You become a representative of the kingdom of God on Earth, bringing to fruition God's purpose in the life of men and women.

Above all the devil is crushed under your feet and you begin to exercise your dominion when you pray. Satan will try to put limitations in your life and make you think that your prayers were not heard by God. Your enemies will encourage you to look to the problems rather than promise and the purpose in your life. He will try to make you focus on your negativities just to limit you. Develop yourself in the spirit of prayer and you will see the salvation of God. Pray until Something Happens in your life (PUSH). Jesus started with prayer and ended with prayer. Prayer is the master key.

So pray and pray - PUSH that dream out and your life will never be the same in Jesus Name.

ONLY YOU CAN PUSH YOURSELF TO SUCCESS THROUGH THE POWER OF PRAYER AND FASTING.

Don't give up in prayer because the devil is not prepared to give in.

CHAPTER SEVEN

GET RID OF NEGATIVE THOUGHTS

'For from within, out of the heart of men, proceed evil thoughts, adulteries, fornications, murders, thefts, covetousness, wickedness, deceit, lasciviousness, an evil eye, blasphemy, pride, foolishness: All these evil things come from within, and defile the man.' **- Mark 7:21-23 King James Version (KJV)**

Do you want to overcome the limitations to your destiny? Are you prepared to say boldly that there are 'no more limits to your destiny'? Then you need to examine yourself and the thoughts that come to your mind daily. We all know that the devil plays a role in limiting us from getting to our sure destiny, but it is also necessary that we check the very thoughts that flow in our mind.

You cannot conquer the devil until you conquer yourself.

Do you know that success is about what you do with your life, because what you think determines your doing? You cannot be a successful person, overcoming the limitations of life, without thinking positively on what you do. The word of God says that 'the way a man thinketh, so shall he become'.

CHAPTER SEVEN

This is to say that you become what you think in life. Your thinking shapes your habits and behaviour.

Anyone who has the habit of procrastinating all the time will never live a life of fulfilment and cannot overcome limitations in life. This is the main reason why you need to start adopting a positive thinking attitude.

From my book 'Igniting the Power of your Creative Mind' you will discover that each and every one of us born into this world is influenced by the things we see, experiences which then determines the way we react to things around us. I have come to appreciate that our parents, our friends, our teachers, our bosses or marriage partners influence our thoughts, knowingly or unknowingly.

According to T D Jakes, once an individual develops certain thoughts in their mind, their mind start to send signals to their emotion which makes them take or make certain decisions or action to produce the outcomes they see.

'Brethren, I count not myself to have apprehended: but this one thing I do, forgetting those things which are behind, and reaching forth unto those things which are before' **- Philippians 3:13**

It is very necessary to note that until an individual renews and changes His or her mind of negative backgrounds or experiences that affected them, their future and dreams are still going to control them, because our mind is influenced by thought from our background being positive or negative.

CHAPTER SEVEN

Everything we do is by choice. If you want to see a change in your personal life, then it is necessary that you change the way you view things. Until you are willing to renew your mind daily, minute by minute changing the way your mind looks at everything with the word of God concerning your destiny, you will see little and your future will be controlled by those negative backgrounds.

'And do not be conformed to this world, but be transformed by the renewing of your mind, that you may prove what is that good and acceptable and perfect will of God.' - **Romans 12:2.**

'The secret of your future is hidden in your daily routine, therefore be careful about what occupies your mind because it will greatly determine what you will become tomorrow' - **Bishop Michael Hutton-Wood**

The terrible truth is that many of us even though we are born again, spirit filled and Holy Ghost talking still live in misery as a result of negative backgrounds we have not let go in our mind and that pulls us backward.

If you do not renew your mindset about your negative experiences you will become depressed and may have suicidal thoughts. Being born again doesn't mean you are going to prevent negative memories coming into your mind or avoid bad and depressing feelings. They are all still going to be there. That is why you need to renew your mind daily with the sure word of God.

CHAPTER SEVEN

Romans 12:1-2 teaches us what we must do: *'I beseech you therefore, brethren, by the mercies of God, that you present your bodies a living sacrifice, holy and acceptable to God. And do not be conformed to this world, but be transformed by the renewing of your mind, that you may prove to be what is good and acceptable and perfect in the will of God.'*

When you were born again God gave you a brand new Godly heart, as Ezekiel tells us: *'Moreover, I will give you a new heart and put a new Spirit within you; and I will remove the heart of stone from your flesh and give you a heart of flesh. And I will put My Spirit within you'*. - **Ezekiel 36:26-27**

However, it is when you combine that new heart with a brand new mindset that awesome and incredible Godly changes will take place in your life and you will be your way to success.

Remember that your mind is the thing that has control over every single action you make. You mind controls your thoughts. Your mind tells your body exactly what to do. It tells your mouth what words to speak. It tells your eyes what to look at. It tells your ears what things to pay attention to and what things to tune out. It tells your brain what to think about. It tells your entire being how to respond in every single situation.

It is also vital that you renew your mindset each day with God's word against bad memories, depressing feelings and everything that takes your focus off God and places it on you and your problems.

CHAPTER SEVEN

Furthermore your mind is the foundation of your intellect, which really controls your personal self-esteem and drives you into success.

It is true that sometimes we are all faced with some thoughts that we have no control over, but you can actually determine which thoughts you hold on to and use to control your lifestyle.

From the book *How to Negotiate your Desired Future with Today's Currency*, by Bishop Michael Hutton-Wood, we discovered that the best way to deal with and forget about your negative experiences is to become fruitful and to occupy yourself with productive thinking to produce something positive. Renewing your mind with the word of God concerning your destiny gives you assurance which then promotes your confidence in your ability to pursue great things in life.

Your background of failures and shortcomings does not matter. When you begin to renew your mindset by changing the way you see yourself, then you can embark on the road to achievement.

'Everyone has a past; but never allow your negative past get in the way of your future.' - **Bishop Michael Hutton-Wood.**

God's promises are always reassuring. He promised to be with us and never to forsake us, to give us victory and rest (Exodus 33:14).

CHAPTER SEVEN

Therefore there is no reason why you should feel intimidated by your negative conditions and not be bold enough to face life like Peter, who dared to walk on the waters.

A wise man once said *'when we see our weakness on our knees, we reap in strength on our feet'*.

'Rejoice not against me, my enemies: when I fall, I shall arise; when I sit in darkness, the LORD shall be a light unto me' - **Micah 7:8**

He who ignores the past is condemned to repeat it. So you must discipline what goes through your mind from the past so as to move on.

Psalm 139 says: *'I will praise the Lord, for I am fearfully and wonderfully made'*. Remind yourself that your birth was not an accident; you were not just born to add to the number of Earth's population. The word of God says that you are a member of a royal priesthood and a special person. You were born to fill a gap, and therefore you are unique.

You have the mind of Christ and all it takes to be great. Just discover who you are in Christ and then you can recover your true self to accomplish greater things.

'For as a man thinketh in his heart, so is he' - **Proverbs 23:7.**

In his book *Think like a Winner!*, Dr Walter Staples writes: 'The key to success lies in your particular manner of thinking. When you change how you think about yourself, your relationships, your goals, and your world, your life changes. If

CHAPTER SEVEN

you change the quality of your thinking, you necessarily will change the quality of your life.'

Be very careful about what you allow to control your mind, about what you think about. What you think about surely becomes your character and identity.

You will not struggle to excel in life and fulfill your purpose on earth in Jesus' name. Learn from the past by all means but be like Apostle Paul: *'One thing I do, forgetting those things which are behind, and reaching forth unto those things which are before'* - **Philippians 3:13.**

Remember also that no matter how hard you try you cannot change the past, but you can definitely make a better future for yourself. Renewal of mind is a non-stop process. Paul says in Ephesians 4:23: 'Be renewed in the spirit of your mind'. We need to work our way through with our minds. The new man always contrasts the old life style, therefore we must make every effort to renew our minds. We should make sure our minds think as it is written in the Word of God. Or else, we need to work on it.

Romans 12:2 says, 'Be not conformed to this world but be transformed by the renewing of your mind'. It is a commandment. Whenever the Bible says 'be', it is a commandment rather than a suggestion. We do not have a choice. The word 'conform' means to assume an outward expression that does not comes from an inward being. In

CHAPTER SEVEN

other words, when you conform to something you feel so much influence that you begin to change the way you act. When you begin to conform to this world system, you are not being faithful to who you really are on the inside. Behind the world system, there is the evil one.

To be transformed is to live an outward expression that comes from the inward being. This transformation needs to take place in our minds. The Bible cautions us that the carnal mind in itself is enmity against God. The transformation comes from the word of God. When you get the word of God out of the pages of your Bible, read it and ponder over it. It will get into your mind and go down into your spirit. When you keep doing this, you can see your mind lining up to your spirit. This is the key. Otherwise, there is this constant battle that goes on between your mind and your spirit.

We all are eternal beings. We have an eternal spirit, we live in a mortal body and we have a soul that is made up of mind, will and emotions. The only doorway for the enemy into your soul is through your mind. Everything starts with a thought. Before you attempt to do anything, you think about it first. Your mind is the doorway to your deeds.

Proverbs 23:7 says, 'As a man thinks in his heart, so is he'. You cannot have a happy life if you have a sad mind. You need a healthy mind to start with. Our mind is the one that makes us the person God made us to be. Ephesians 6:12 says, ' We

CHAPTER SEVEN

do not wrestle against flesh and blood, but against principalities, against powers, against the evil rulers of this dark world'.

It is so important to guard our thought life. Isaiah 26:3 says, 'If you will keep your mind stayed on Me, I will hold you in perfect peace'.

Situations and circumstances change all the time. If our minds stay on the things that are changing day to day, our life will be like a boat in a storm. That is why it is so important we have an anchor. You will never wage a successful battle unless you have a personal relationship with the Lord Jesus Christ.

If you desire a meaningful and successful life, then you must begin to rid your mind of the negative and embrace your future. These negatives or 'little foxes' could be what are limiting you from getting to your destiny. *'Take us the foxes, the little foxes that spoil the vines: for our vines have tender grapes.'* **- Song of Solomon 2:15**

'Life is never made unbearable by circumstances, but only by lack of meaning and purpose.' **- Viktor Frankl**

The story was told of a teenage girl who visited a zoo with her friends. As they went past a particular cage, she stopped and gazed at a huge animal, but she was not sure what type of animal it was. She asked her friends to look at the other animals while she concentrated on this one.

Amazingly, as she got closer to the animal, the teenage girl

CHAPTER SEVEN

realized that it was a group of elephants being held by a thin rope tied to their legs. The girl was very confused. Such big and powerful animals could at any time break away from the rope they were tied to, but for some strange reason they did not. She looked around and saw a trainer nearby, so she asked him why these huge and magnificent elephants just stood there and made no attempt to break free from the rope.

The trainer responded to the confused teenage girl and said 'When these elephants were very little, we used the same rope size to tie them down. It's enough to hold them for as long as they decide to keep them. As the elephants grow up, they are conditioned to believe they can't break free'. The girl was amazed that the elephants could not break away and that they believed they were stuck right where they were.

The lesson here is that these powerful and gigantic creatures are unable to break free from their past limitations. Like the elephants, how many of us go through life holding on to a negative belief that we cannot go beyond barriers and limitations, simply because we have been told that we cannot make it in life, or have failed at something before?

Have you refused to attempt something new and challenging because of your limited mindset, due to your past? No matter what limited you in the past, or how poor your background was, neglected or downtrodden, you have what it takes to be at the top.

CHAPTER SEVEN

'For as a man thinketh in his heart, so is he' - **Proverbs 23:7**

It is my fervent prayer that as you begin to renew your mindset about your life you will be like the stars, which do not struggle to shine, or as a river, which does not struggle to flow. You will get to your destiny. Amen.

CHAPTER EIGHT

PURSUE, OVERTAKE AND RECOVER YOUR DESTINY

'And David inquired at the LORD, saying, Shall I pursue after this troop? Shall I overtake them? And he answered him, Pursue: for thou shalt surely overtake them, and without fail recover all.'
- **1 Samuel 30:8 (NKJ)**

Did you know that our Heavenly Father created and placed great potential within us to become all that we can be to maximize our sure destiny? When you look at an apple for example, there are seeds within that fruit, but they are not visible until you open up the fruit. That means the apple has the potential to replenish, multiply and increase, as long as that seed is discovered and not destroyed. The seed is unlimited as long as it is planted in the right soil and remains planted. The word of God says that *'it shall be like a tree planted by the rivers of water; it will bring forth its fruit in its season, whose leaf also will not wither'* - **Psalms 1:3**

As long as you remain planted in the word of God, nothing should stop you from pursuing your destiny. It does not matter about your negative background in education, family breakdown, lack of finances or immigration issues, you have the potential to be great in life. Nothing will stop you if you discover what to do with the word of God that breaks all barriers and removes limitation from your destiny.

Stop limiting your own destiny by looking at those setbacks, failures and disappointments and focusing on the Lord Jesus Christ, who is able to do all things and will empower you to that sure future, if you do not lose heart.

Let me assure you that your God knows your future better than you can imagine and that He has planted a purpose within you that is bigger than the negative experiences trying to limit you. You are unique in the sight of God, and that is the main reason why He gave you the purpose you have. Just pursue that vision or purpose and your life will never be the same. Remember that you only pursue your destiny through the power of faith. The Bible made it clear that *'for without faith it is impossible to please God'*.

Faith gives you stability and grace empowers you to become.

In Genesis 27, we saw in the lives of two brothers in the Bible, Esau and Jacob, how both of them were faced with different limitations but broke through those limitations. We saw how Esau became very restless and tried to take whatever belonged to him in life. Jacob, even though he fled with his brother's blessing, travailed in prayer and demanded a change of story and a change of name.

CHAPTER EIGHT

The Bible gave an account in Genesis 28:11-13 that *'he came to a certain place and stayed there all night, because the sun had set. And he took one of the stones of that place and put it at his head, and lay down in that place to sleep. Then he dreamed, and behold a ladder was set on the earth, and its top reached to heaven; and there the angels of God were ascending and descending on it'*. Here we saw that Jacob had a vision or a dream that connected him to the heavenly, and as he made his mind to pursue that dream, there were no limits as to how much he could get from Heaven, and his status in life was transformed.

What has the Lord shown you in your dream (your purpose) for the assignment on Earth? Is your purpose in life connected to Heaven or disconnected, making your life miserable or confused?

What is your purpose here in life? Why are you here on earth? God might have a purpose for your life, but you are being limited by negative situations, barriers or closed doors. You have the potential to be the head in that department, for that promotion, for the business, yet it's being passed on to somebody else.

You may have prayed like Jacob, and perhaps the Lord had revealed to you a particular business that you are destined to be the head of, but you are being limited by evil attacks or family demons who have decided that you will not be the head but the tail. This may be placing limitations from getting to your destiny. However, the good news is that you will not be limited any more as you discover who you are in the word of God. No weapon that is against you shall ever prosper.

'And David inquired of the Lord, saying, Shall I pursue after this troupe? Shall I overtake them? And he answered him, Pursue, for thou shalt surely overtake them, and without fail recover all.'
- 1 Samuel 30: 8

We observed from the Bible verses that for you to become all that God has created you to be in life you have three very important things to do in order to fulfil your assignment or purpose. They are to *Pursue*, to *Overtake* and to *Recover*.

This is to say that for you to be able to chase your purpose in life as a soldier who is on a battlefront, you need to have these three characters. Every soldier knows that when his enemies have kidnapped a fellow soldier he must pursue them until he and his comrades overcome them, and then recover or rescue the soldier from the enemy camp. So perhaps you are destined to be great in life, but the enemies of progress have taken your ideas, resources, vision, purpose, children, marriage, education, business plan or the growth of your ministry into captivity. How do you get those things back from the hands of your visible and invisible enemies? You need to be determined that you are going to *pursue*, *overtake* and then *recover* your future from the belly of the destiny destroyers.

CHAPTER EIGHT

'I have pursued mine enemies, and overtaken them: neither did I turn again till they were consumed.' - **Psalms 18: 37**

Remember that you are a soldier in the army of the Lord, and you cannot overtake without running or chasing the destiny destroyers, because they have made their minds up to run away with your dreams. You need to chase after them until you corner them and claim back that which they have stolen from you.

You cannot become a hero or champion in life without developing the habit of pursuing, overtaking and recovering.

The Bible is littered with about 92,000,000 promises for you, but you cannot claim them without doing something to provoke them. If you obey the Lord and serve him, then you shall spend your days in pleasures and prosperity.

In Joshua 1:8, we discovered that *'This book of the law shall not depart from thy mouth, but you shall meditate in it day and night, that you may observe to do (not to quote) according to all that is written in it. For then you will make your way prosperous and then you will have good success'*.

God always wants a relationship with you. He wants a family relationship, as he is our father. God has a purpose and a plan for our lives. In Hebrews 10:7 we learn that we are created for a specific purpose, and we identify that purpose and plan for our lives. However, there is a need to plan by actually sitting down and counting the cost involved in the

CHAPTER EIGHT

dream. Having a dream, plan, and vision alone is not enough, but counting the cost is another thing all together. *'For who of you, willing to build a tower, doth not first, having sat down, count the expenses, whether he has the things for completing?'*

So the question here is, what is having a vision for life? During my research, I came across different meanings of vision. Some define it as having a purpose, goal or dream, while others differentiate between vision and purpose.

To be able to live a life full of impact, it is very important that you discover your purpose for living and do every positive thing to see it come true.

'You don't only have to have a dream but to chase it to its limits and make sure you catch it' - **Barack Hussain Obama, President of United States of America.**

In this chapter I will be looking at vision as purpose, to drive home what we really want to understand. Having a vision or purpose for your life means being determined or persuaded to do or achieve something positive through definitive decision-making.

'But Daniel purposed in his heart that he would not defile himself with the portion of the king's meat, nor with the wine which he drank: therefore he requested the prince of the eunuchs that he might not defile himself' - **Daniel 1:8**

Having a dream or goal set before you means keeping your eyes on that goal and going in that direction. It means not

CHAPTER EIGHT

being easily distracted by any sounds or individuals along the way to fulfill your purpose. Having made your mind to stand alone and firm, whether somebody encourages or promotes you or not, you make a conscious decision to see that dream come to pass in your life.

'Don't chase your pension, chase your dream passion' - **unknown**

A purposeful person is one who is able to stand on the truth. He buys the truth and sells it not. He is an individual who has made up his mind to hold on to the truth and withstand evil. He is not moved by the winds of distractors but keeps sailing in the direction in which he has to overcome. To be able to succeed in life and influence nations, you need to deny yourself certain things that do not correspond with your purpose. You need to deny yourself pleasures, because you know your purpose for your life and focus on your dream.

In Daniel 1:8 we saw that he has a purpose for his life: *'But Daniel purposed in his heart that he would not defile himself with the portion of the king's meat, nor with the wine which he drank: therefore he requested of the prince of the eunuchs that he might not defile himself'*.

Daniel's purpose or vision was not to defile himself with the king's meat. He knew that the consequences of not eating the king's meat were great, but he denied himself in order to please

CHAPTER EIGHT

God. He was in Babylon alone with his principles and the determination to stand for that purpose. His parents were not there to assure him, neither were there any other family members to persuade him to comply with the customs of Babylon.

It is very important that we stand by our visions and the dreams we have. There may be dangers around you to persuade you to go against your purpose, but hold on to that purpose and the dream. In the process of time, if you work smartly, you will achieve it.

'While we look not at the things which are seen, but at the things which are not seen: for the things which are seen are temporal; but the things which are not seen are eternal' - **2 Corinthians 4:18.**

If you are not moved by challenges, the discouragement of loved ones and the devil's tricks to abort your dream, you will realize that those challenges were nothing compare to your fulfilment in life.

You make your mind up to hold unto God's promises through his word, that nothing can separate you from your purpose and you will achieve the purpose for which that dream was given to you. You need to encourage yourself in the Lord, as David did in his days. Habakkuk 2:1-3 states: *'I will stand upon my watch, and set me upon the tower, and will watch to see what he will say unto me, and what I shall answer when I am reproved. And the LORD answered me, and said, write the vision, and make it plain upon tables, that he may run that*

CHAPTER EIGHT

readeth it. For the vision is yet for an appointed time, but at the end it shall speak, and not lie: though it tarry, wait for it; because it will surely come, it will not tarry'.

There is a need to watch and pray concerning your purpose and dreams and to ensure that it drives your spirit daily, because there is a tendency to lose focus on that dream. You need to protect and guide your purpose, because not many people out there are happy about your dreams of achieving those grades in the university, attaining a new contract for your business, buying or building a ideal home or finding your perfect marriage partner. There are still 'pharaohs' in the present day who are looking to destroy your baby, your dream.

Let me tell you a story about a young man named Joseph. His father's name was Jacob, and they lived in Canaan, where his grandfather was from. A time came in Joseph's life when he became a teenager. He was seventeen and had eleven brothers, ten of them older and one younger than him. His father spent more time with him because he was one of the youngest sons, and he became very special to him.

In the process of time as this young teenager grew, his father Jacob had a special robe made for him. It was very beautiful and had all the colours of the rainbow. His older brothers saw this and got very jealous, because they thought his father liked him more than them.

There came a point in Joseph's life when he had a dream,

CHAPTER EIGHT

a purpose, a vision, a goal, and he went and told his brothers about it. He dreamed that as they were tying up sheaves of grain out in the field his suddenly stood up, while all theirs gathered around and bowed to him. Positive as the dream was to Joseph, it was not received well by his brothers. The brothers looked at each other in disgust, but Joseph continued.

'Then I had another dream, that the sun, moon and eleven stars bowed down to me' he said.

'Who do you think you are?' the brothers asked him. 'Do you think you are better than all of us? Do you think we would ever bow down to you?'

It had made the brothers dislike Joseph even more. That is why you need to be very careful who share your dreams, visions, ideas, and goals with.

When Joseph told his father about his dreams Jacob said, 'Those are strange dreams.' But he thought carefully about what Joseph had told him. Any time you have a dream or vision about your future, share it with your spiritual father (your God-appointed pastor), who will pray with you, encourage you and stand with you to see that dream come to pass.

A few days later Joseph's father asked him to check on his brothers whilst they were in the fields quite a distance away, so Joseph went to find them. When the brothers saw Joseph in the distance, they made a plan to kill him. But when Reuben, Joseph's oldest brother, heard this he said, 'Let's not

CHAPTER EIGHT

kill him. Let's just throw him in a well out here in the field.' Reuben said this because he was secretly planning to come back and rescue Joseph when the other brothers had left. So when Joseph came to them, they took off his beautiful robe and they threw him in an empty well.

A little while later a group of people came by who wanted to sell some things in Egypt. One of the brothers spoke up. 'Why don't we sell him to these people? He said. 'This way we never have to see him again, and we don't have to kill him.' The other brothers liked this idea, so they sold him to the people who were going to Egypt.

Unfortunately Reuben had been working, and hadn't seen what had happened. When he returned to the well he saw that Joseph was gone. He had been sold to an important man named Potiphar, an assistant to the Pharaoh of Egypt.

The rest of the brothers took Joseph's beautiful robe, dipped it in animal blood and took it back to their father. When Jacob saw this he cried, 'Some animal has killed my son!' He cried for many days, so much that nobody could comfort him.

Now Joseph had started out as a slave, but the Lord was with Joseph and He helped him do everything right. So Potiphar made him his helper, and put him in charge of everything he owned. The problem came when Potiphar's wife lied about Joseph to her husband, so Potiphar had Joseph put into jail.

CHAPTER EIGHT

The Lord was still with Joseph in jail, and the warden put him in charge of all the prisoners. He never worried, because the Lord was with Joseph and helped him do everything right.

After Joseph had been in jail for some time, a cupbearer and baker to Pharaoh were sent there. One night each of them had a dream. They told their dreams to Joseph and he told the cupbearer that he would soon be let out of jail.

'Please tell Pharaoh about me, and ask him to get me out of here' Joseph said. But when the cupbearer was freed he forgot about what Joseph had said, so Joseph stayed in jail for two more years.

Then one day Pharaoh had a dream, and nobody could explain it to him. But the cupbearer then remembered what Joseph had done for him, and Joseph was brought to Pharaoh.

'Can you understand dreams?' Pharaoh asked.

'I can't, but God helps me' Joseph replied. After Pharaoh had told him his dream Joseph explained, 'God is warning you. There will be seven years when nothing will grow and there won't be any food for anyone.'

'What can I do?' Pharaoh asked.

'God has shown you what to do' replied Joseph. 'There will be seven years before the bad years that will be very good. So you should save a little of each year's harvest. That way you will have enough to get you through the bad years.'

Pharaoh believed all that Joseph told him, and put him in charge of all the land of Egypt.

CHAPTER EIGHT

People came from all countries to buy grain from Joseph, because the whole world was in need of food. Some of those people were Joseph's brothers. When his brothers came, Joseph recognized them, but they did not know who he was. (It had been over 10 years since they had last seen him).

The brothers all bowed to him, because he was an important person, just as he had dreamed they would at the beginning. After a few meetings with his brothers he could not keep it in any longer and said to them, 'I am Joseph! Is my father alive?'

His brothers couldn't answer him because they were afraid. Then Joseph said, 'Come here. I am your brother, the one you sold! Do not worry, and do not be angry at yourselves for selling me, because God has put me here to save people from starving.'

So his father, his brothers, and their families came to live in Egypt with Joseph, and they had all the food they needed.

The conclusion of this long story is that you should beware who you share dreams with. However, if you have shared them with people you call loved ones and you are suffering as a result of it, there is hope for you. No matter the consequences of your sharing that dream, God is your protector; he will protect you and your dreams will be realized.

'*Life without a purpose is life without meaning. The greatest tragedy in life is not death, but life without purpose*' - **Dr Myles Munroe.**

CHAPTER EIGHT

I humorously say that a meaningless life is worse than cancer.

'Trust in the LORD with all thine heart; and lean not unto thine own understanding. In all thy ways acknowledge him, and he shall direct thy paths.' - **Proverbs 3:5-6**

In pursuit of your purpose, dream or vision it is very important that you identify your personal strengths and weaknesses. By so doing you identify the necessary steps needed to actually see that purpose being fulfilled. You cannot say that you have a dream and do not know what, when and how that dream can be achieved.

You need to have knowledge about what to do regarding that vision. Many of us are destroyed, even though we have dreams and ambition; we lack the knowledge which is the power for success.

'My people are destroyed for lack of knowledge: because thou hast rejected knowledge.' - **Hosea 4:6.**

'Give me now wisdom and knowledge that I may go out and come in before this people: for who can judge this thy people that is so great?' - **2 Chronicles 1:10.**

Solomon needed knowledge in pursuing his vision, a goal, a purpose in life as a king. He knew that without knowledge and a discerning heart to govern God's people, he would not be able to distinguish between right and wrong (strengths and weaknesses) (Isaiah 40:29)

I heard my Bishop say 'The future is secured by those who

know how to sharpen and use their gifts and their strength by identifying and making the most of their given opportunities.'

'Patiently wait on the Lord to be all that He has purposed for you in this world. He that committeth sin is of the devil; for the devil sinneth from the beginning. For this purpose the Son of God was manifested, that he might destroy the works of the devil.' - **1 John 3:8 and Psalms 27:14**

'Your value of knowledge determines your up-liftment in life' - **David Oyedepo (Junior).**

Decisiveness of purpose is characterized by firmness of the vision and goal you have decided to pursue in life. However, as believers we need to understand that decisiveness does not mean being stubborn, arrogant or hasty but the ability to decide with speed and clarity in all matters of life.

Ruth in her journey with her mother-in-law made her mind to follow regardless of the price involved. *'And Ruth said, intreat me not to leave thee, or to return from following after thee: for whither thou goest, I will go; and where thou lodgest, I will lodge: thy people shall be my people, and thy God my God: Where thou diest, will I die, and there will I be buried: the LORD do so to me, and more also, if ought but death part thee and me'* - **Ruth 1:16-17, Psalms 112:7-8**

Ruth was very determined to follow even to the point of death. She had a purpose and a will regardless of persuasion. She spoke with confidence to remain with her definite purpose steadfastly. Samuel also had the courage to remain faithful to his conviction and purpose (1 Samuel 2:26).

Jeremiah was another example who stood for the purpose he had to preach the word of the Lord. He decided not to turn back from his visions, goals and the direction he had (Jeremiah 26:12). He was also not concerned with what the people of that nation would do to him. He was ready to pay the painful price and go through self-denial to bring his purpose to pass. We have to be able to deny ourselves at all times in achieving our purpose in life.

Being decisive is simply the most rational way to take on any problem. You observe the information you have available and then you decide what would be the most successful course of action. If it is possible to get more information, you decide how to get it. If you can't get more data, you simply decide with the facts available.

'Without a decision no progress can be made' - **Bishop Hutton-Wood.**

Although it would be nice if we lived in a world where perfect information can be retrieved readily, being decisive ultimately means recognizing when you already have the best information you are going to get.

At this point you simply need to make a decision with the information at hand and move forward. Waiting longer is just delaying the inevitable, so you must decide in the face of uncertainty.

CHAPTER EIGHT

The word of God cannot lie; what he has promised concerning your destiny he will do. In every believer's hands, there lie the seeds of failure or potential for greatness. Your decision regarding your purpose will only be realized if you are decisive and remain focused.

'Be like a postage stamp on a letter to your destination' - **Unknown**

I have come to appreciate that 'Success is by choice and failure is by choice'. All great men and successful people in life make choices, and those choices are either to promote their business or let it collapse.

In the pursuit of our individual dreams we need to make the choice not to give up along the way but remain focused on our particular dreams, business, goals and studies to see them come to pass. Until we really concentrate in our purpose in life we cannot be successful.

When all attention, time and effort is given to your dreams and purpose you will experience God's extraordinary favours and miracles in your life. It is also very important that we fight to remain focused and decisive in anything you set your mind on by building walls that will strengthen your concentration.

Intimidation and bullying are both methods others use to get you to change your mind or your stance on your purpose. Be like the three Hebrews boys, Shadrach, Meshach and Abednego, who made the choice to remain focused and never

CHAPTER EIGHT

give in to intimidation to defile almighty God. Unless you pursue your studies, business and training and are diligent, your life will remain stuck in the same spot.

You cannot overtake those who have gone before you in business, career, marriage etc. God will always answer the prayer you prayed in faith. He cannot answer you unless you go to the throne room of prayer. With bended knee, the Lord God will answer as He did in the life of Hannah.

Many things have been stolen from us the believers and are kept in the store room of destiny destroyers. It about time that we got restless and engaged in fervent prayer to recover all that has been stolen from us; there will always be limitations over your destiny. Genesis 27:40 made it clear that there is the need for restlessness in life to pursue, overtake and recover all. Esau became restless and broke the yoke of limitations over his neck.

CHAPTER NINE

TRUST IN THE LORD

'But those who wait on the LORD shall renew their strength; they shall mount up with wings like eagles, they shall run and not be weary, they shall walk and not faint' - **Isaiah 40:31**

Trusting God in the face of total defeat is perhaps the ultimate test of patience in the Christian life. Nobody wants to be friends with a loser, as Job found out through rejection and terrible trial by fire. Yet when he learned to stand still and wait upon the LORD, he found restoration.

When David and his men found that their wives and children had been taken captive, *'David was greatly distressed; for the people spake of stoning him, because the soul of all the people was grieved, every man for his sons and for his daughters: but David encouraged himself in the LORD his God'* - **1 Samuel 30:6**. David had learned how to stand still and wait upon the LORD. Soon every wife, child and piece of property was recovered without damage.

There can be no reason to doubt, while you wait upon God; nor can doubting do you the least good. Hope will cheer you, brighten your prospects, and save you from despondency and gloom. Therefore hope in the Lord. You may be deeply tried, severely exercised, and at times almost overwhelmed; but at the very worst, you should expostulate with yourself, and say 'Why are you cast down, O my soul? And why are you disturbed within me? Hope in God; for I shall yet praise him for the help of his countenance.'

However rough your road, however violent the conflict, however severe the trial, still hope on, hope always; for God has said 'They shall not be ashamed, who wait for me.' Like a vessel on the ocean, you may have to meet with storms and tempests; you may be tossed and tumbled about, but hope will be as an anchor of the soul, both sure and steadfast, and which enters into that within the veil, 'Therefore, let Israel hope in the Lord; for with the Lord there is mercy, and with him is plenteous redemption.'

Never give up, while you need a blessing, fear a foe, or groan under a burden. Wait on the Lord until you obtain all you need, and enjoy all you desire. You cannot wait on him in vain; therefore you cannot do better. Satan will suggest 'Why should you wait for the Lord any longer?' Tell him that your God is a Sovereign, and will work in his own time and way; tell him you are a poor, dependent creature, and must not dictate to the Most High; tell him that he has appeared for thousands before you, and that he will appear for you. Let

CHAPTER NINE

Satan suggest what he may, let doubts rise thick, let fears come strong, still wait on the Lord. It is your plain duty, it is your only hope, and it is your sure resource.

Plead with God and take no denial, rest on the promise of God and never give it up. Wait at the throne of God, and let nothing drive you thence. If the Lord seems to be turned against you, and if everything seems to conspire to discourage you, still persevere. Remember the woman of Canaan, how she was discouraged; but she persevered and succeeded. Remember Jacob, how he was discouraged, and yet succeeded. Remember Moses, to whom God said 'Let me alone', but he persevered and succeeded. Remember Hezekiah, what a death-blow he got, but he persevered and succeeded. The Lord will turn again; he will have compassion upon you; for he will cast all your sins into the depths of the sea. Trust, then, in the Lord forever, for in the Lord Jehovah there is everlasting strength; and that strength shall be put forth, and be made perfect in your weakness.

With God all things are possible and nothing is too hard for him to do for you only if you can trust and depend on Him. Your case could be as bad and terrible as the poor woman in the Gospel who had spent all her money, tried all the physicians, and yet her life was no better. Things rather grew worse, until she came to Jesus for a change of her situation and status. The good news was that she obtained supernatural

CHAPTER NINE

healing after twelve years of pain and isolation from society. What is your situation? Just trust in the Lord and he will give you the desires of your life.

'*For whatsoever is born of God overcometh the world: and this is the victory that overcometh the world, even our faith*' - **1 John 5:4**

No matter what limitations are thrown at you do not limit GOD. Trust in the Lord always and He will direct your path into greatness. David said in psalm 23:4, '*Yea though I walk through the valley of the shadow of death, I will fear no evil. For you are with me. Your rod and staff they comfort me.*'

No matter how terrible your case may be, it does not matter if you have been rejected by society or family members, educational institutions or marriage breakdown, just look unto Jesus. He is a waymaker, and he will make a way for you. Trust in the Lord. Do not lean on your own understanding, because your understanding is limited, but His plans for your life will come to pass in your life.

No more limits to your destiny.

CHAPTER TEN

WALK BY FAITH

'We walk by faith, not by sight' - **2 Corinthians 5:7**

Faith is the act of trusting, hoping and believing in the goodness and trustworthiness of God. Therefore, walking by faith simply means believing that whatever the word of God says concerning you is true and without evidence engaging the act of seeing, that thing will come to pass in your life.

'Faith is being obedient to what you believe you were called to do and sure of what we hope for and certain of what we do not see' - **Hebrews 11:1**

To believe in something and not doing anything to see that thing manifest in your life is not acting or taking the step of faith. After you have believed in something positive about your future, it is therefore your full responsibility to act, work, make and to deploy your senses to have what you wanted.

The word of God clearly states that 'without faith, it is impossible to please God' (Hebrews 11:6)

'Faith is taking the first step, even when you don't see the whole staircase' - **Martin Luther King Jr, US black civil rights leader & clergyman (1929 - 1968)**

CHAPTER TEN

Discovering purpose, dreams and vision about you alone is not enough; you must actually take positive steps to see those dreams come true. You may have had a negative background or horrible circumstances when you were growing up and therefore those events may be very hurtful in your memory; you need to take steps to avoid those events repeating in your life, you need to make a conscious decision to put measures in place to prevent them happening. You have the power to change things to favour you by developing your confidence and belief in the word of God concerning you.

'To accomplish great things, we must dream as well as act' - **Anatole France, French novelist (1844 - 1924)**

Knowing the importance of water to your body and that it is very good for your kidneys, yet not taking the step to go and get the water to drink is not acting on your knowledge. That is not faith either.

'Any faith that makes God fully responsible is irresponsible faith' - **Dr David Oyedepo**

Faith without work is dead. Whatever and wherever you are now is subject to change, if you are not happy with the situation. No condition is permanent. It takes the step of faith to pray to God to see a result. You may have had a bad and terrible upbringing, but once you discover that you are not very happy about your life, you can act on God's word for your life and do positive things to turn events to your favour.

CHAPTER TEN

Your life may be boring because you made it that way. When was the last time you tried something really difficult? When was the last time you challenged the odds by doing something risky? Do it now.

'And we know that all things work together for good to them that love God, to them who are called according to his purpose' - **Romans 8:28**

God has a purpose for your life and the gate of hell cannot stop you from achieving that goal. It does not matter about your family background what other people say, you will be successful in Jesus' Name.

'Do not laugh at me, my enemies. Although I've fallen, I will get up. Although I sit in the dark, the LORD is my light' - **Micah 7:8.**

By faith Abraham, when called to go to a place he would later receive as his inheritance, obeyed and went, even though he did not know where he was going. By faith he made his home in the Promised Land like a stranger in a foreign country; he lived in tents, as did Isaac and Jacob, who were heirs with him to the same promise.

'For he was looking forward to the city with foundations, whose architect and builder is God' - **Hebrews 11:8-10**

In order to take the steps of faith, there is the need to read the word of God concerning you. Faith comes by hearing, and hearing by the word of God. You hear God's word activate your joy inside you to hold on to His sure promises for your destiny.

CHAPTER TEN

This is say that faith in God's word produces inner joy.

'These things have I spoken unto you, that my joy might remain in you, and that your joy might be full' - **John 15:11**

'My brethren, count it all joy when ye fall into divers temptation; knowing this, that the trying of your faith worketh patience' - **James 1:2-3**

'However, faith is nothing unless we live it out, and without faith it is impossible to please God' - **Hebrews 11:6**

So no matter what you are going through in life as a result of your negative history or background, the word of God encourages you to count it all joy, because joy is the driving force to victory in Jesus' Name. Adversity will come, but it is only those who have maintained their joy who enjoy the victory.

Your circumstances may be showing negatives, but remember that God has not left you or forsaken you. It is your attitude and the steps of faith you take in God's word against those negative backgrounds that will empower you to overcome and have a fruitful future. *'Go your way, eat the fat, and drink the sweet, and send portions unto them for whom nothing is prepared: for this day is holy unto our Lord: neither be ye sorry; for the joy of the LORD is your strength'* - **Nehemiah 8:9**

Without struggle, you cannot and will not ever develop your potential. Have you ever watched an ant carrying home a piece of bread that is bigger than he is? *'Success belongs to those who are too small to carry what they believe in; but too big to leave it behind'* - **unknown**

CHAPTER TEN

If God the creator lives within you, then you are creative. That means that when you cannot find a job, you take the step of faith to go out there and look for or create your own job. In other words, if success does not come to you, get up and go after it.

Be a soldier. Give yourself orders and follow them. Instill some rough and unquestioned discipline in your life. Get up early in the morning, do your work as if you're on a battlefield and then go to sleep. Repeat until your problems become just situations you can solve by following an easy sequence of new orders.

'You don't only have to have a dream but to chase it to its limits'
- Barack Hussain Obama, President of the United States of America

It was reported that one day a young man asked his father, 'What is the secret of your success?' 'Good decisions' his father replied. 'How did you learn to make good decisions?' The young man asked. 'By making bad ones' the father replied.

Once you discover your purpose, dreams and gifts, take the step of faith and go and develop those dreams and gifts into fulfilment. Do not wait for an opportunity, because the opportunity is the breath in your body and the strength in mind. That is why renewing of the mind is necessary for your destiny (see **Romans 12:1-2**).

In Deuteronomy 8:18, we discovered that God does not give us wealth but empowers us to get it. Taking the step of

CHAPTER TEN

faith forbids you from sitting down and waiting for God to drop everything on your lap.

I heard Bishop David Oyedepo once say 'Success does not fall on people's laps but comes through the act of faith and self development'. This is to say, a dream without a definite corresponding action only irritates and aggravates the soul and amounts to nothing. It does not matter what happened to you in the past; if you can begin to renew your mind and take the step of faith to create the future you really want, then God will give you the power to succeed.

Take the step of faith in believing God's word concerning you rather than what men have said in your life. This will surely increase your joy and empower you to see what the Lord God has promised you. Refuse to allow your background to hinder, prevent, stop or limit you from achieving your full potential. Reject any form of rejection from family and friends and see God as the only one who can secure your destiny.

Nevertheless, faith does not mean sitting and waiting every day for an answer. It doesn't just mean believing God will provide, or God will show you the way. It means taking an actual 'step of faith' in the direction you believe God is leading you.

'There is surely a future hope for you, and your hope will not be cut off' - **Proverbs 23:18 (NIV).**

'Be of good courage, and he shall strengthen your heart, all ye that hope in the LORD' - **Psalms 31:24 (KJV)**

CHAPTER TEN

Put a big smile on your face always and begin to rejoice in the Lord.

Maybe you did something really wrong, and your current situation is the result of that mistake. Take responsibility, but don't blame yourself. It's all in the past. You are in the present now and you can do something about it. Blame will only put weight on that past and drag you down.

'The only limit to our realization of tomorrow will be our doubts of today. Let us move forward with strong and active faith' - **unknown**

You are born to be a winner and you cannot be defeated when you take the step of faith to develop yourself in God's word and engage in some practical steps in developing yourself to where you want to be. The devil is a liar, and he will not win. YOU are the winner.

CHAPTER ELEVEN

DEVELOPING THE ATTITUDE OF GRATITUDE

1Thessalonians 5: 18; Ephesians 5: 20; Philippians 4: 6; Colossians 33: 17

'Develop an attitude of gratitude, and give thanks for everything that happens to you, knowing that every step forward is a step toward achieving something bigger and better than your current situation.' - **Brian Tracy**

Developing the attitude of gratitude means to adopt a lifestyle of thanksgiving and to be able to show appreciation to someone you revere highly for what they have done for you. Your attitude remains the same irrespective of the circumstances facing you. You still appreciate God for the life you have.

Your attitude is that no matter what limitations before you, you will make your mind up to remain grateful. Sometimes negative thoughts and ideas may arise to challenge your love for God, but you develop the habit to remain thankful at all times.

In everything give thanks, for this is the will of God in Christ

CHAPTER ELEVEN

concerning you. 'Let the high praises of God be in their mouth, and a two-edged sword in their hand, to execute vengeance upon the heathen, and punishments upon the people, to bind their kings with chains, and their nobles with fetters of iron, to execute upon them the judgments written, this honour have all his saints, praise ye the Lord' - **Psalms 149: 6-9**

'I will trust him whatever, wherever I am, I can never be thrown away. If I am in sickness, my sickness may serve Him, in perplexity, my perplexity may serve Him, if I am in sorrow my serve Him. My sickness or perplexity or sorrow may be necessary causes of some great end, which is quite beyond us. He does nothing in vain.' - **John Henry Newman**

'The vine is dried up, and the fig tree languisheth, the pomegranate tree, the palm tree also , and the apple tree, even all the tress of the field, are withered, because joy is withered away from the sons of men' - **Joel 1:1-2**

'Seeds of discouragement will not grow in a thankful heart' - **Anonymous**

When we lack the spirit of thankfulness and praises to God for the things we have now, even the little we have is taken away from us. Anything we may set our hands on may become dried up. We may lack freshness in our marriage, simply because we lack joy and gratitude. It is very important that we maintain the heart of gratefulness always, as it brings things faster to us.

CHAPTER ELEVEN

The Bible says 'The joy of the Lord is my strength'. My Bishop once made a statement which really cracked up my brain. According to him 'gratefulness is a covenant attitude', which is very true.

Given that we are children of the great Jehovah, we have a covenant with Him regarding our salvation, so it is important and prudent that we maintain the covenant attitude of gratitude towards him, with the appreciation that God is still and always will be in control – see Luke 12:22-23

A joyful attitude of thanksgiving brings things our way even if we do not seem to qualify for them. It is my personal observation that when we lose our sense of gratitude, we can lose our peace and joy, for our God desires that we enjoy peace and joy at all times – see Romans 8:28. As David puts it: 'I will praise the name of God with a song; I will magnify him with thanksgiving'.

'This will please the Lord more than an ox or a bull with horns and hoofs; Let the oppressed see it and be glad. You, who seek God, let your hearts revive' - **Psalms 69: 30-32**

The accounts of Paul and Silas as recorded in Acts 16:23-26 is quite revealing: *'And when they had laid many stripes upon them, they cast them into prison, charging the jailor to keep them safely, who having received such a charge thrust them into the inner prison, and made their feet fast in the stocks. And at midnight Paul and Silas prayed and sang praises unto God, and the prisoners*

CHAPTER ELEVEN

heard them and suddenly there was a great earthquake, so that the foundations of the prison were shaken, and immediately all the doors were opened, and every one's bands were loosed'.

Paul and Silas, as we are told, were arrested and put in prison for casting a spirit of divination out of a girl. They were subjected to severe torture, but nevertheless, in the midst of their suffering and pain, they prayed and sang praises to God. This may sound ridiculous and strange to the other prisoners, who were used to hearing only the groans and cries of beaten and tortured prisoners.

In the process of time the earthquake that shook the foundations of the prison flung its doors open and not only were the bonds of Paul and Silas released but those of the other inmates.

A question that may come to mind may be - what had caused the prison doors to open? Surely, praise and worship is the answer. Praise and worship lift us to the presence of God.

'There is fullness of joy in the presence of God' - **Deuteronomy 4:29**

It is important that we recognize the presence of God who created all that we have and will ever need. Paul and Silas no doubt were aware of the power of praise and worship, how to lift their hearts above their challenges or problems and enter into the presence and power of almighty God, hence they engaged God's power through praise and worship and this

CHAPTER ELEVEN

brought them into his peace and presence, opening the door of opportunity for the Heavenly Father to help them.

The Bible makes it clear that God lives in the praises of his people (Psalm 22: 3). In other words, God 'dwells' in the atmosphere of praises. Thus praise is not merely a reaction to coming into the presence of our maker, but a vehicle of faith which brings us in to the presence and power of the great Jehovah. Praise and worship is a 'gate pass' which allows us entry into the sacredness of his glory.

The psalmist will say *'Enter into his gates with thanksgiving and into his courts with praise, be thankful unto him, and bless his name'* - **Psalm 100:4**

Our Lord and saviour Jesus Christ also emphasizes the need to value the presence of God when it comes to praise and worship, *'for where two or three are gathered together in my name, there am I in their midst'* - **Matthew 18: 20**. It is also important that whenever we gather to praise his name, our God should be our only focus of everything we preach and sing about. *'I will declare thy name unto my brethren, in the midst of the church will l sing and praise unto thee'* - **Hebrews 2:12.**

It is interesting to note that miracles can manifest in the atmosphere of praise and worship as God's power responds when we invoke his presence into our lives through this medium.

Praising God actually means 'to command, applaud or magnify'. It is an expression of worship, lifting up and glorifying the living Lord. It is an act of humility, focusing our attention upon the Lord, with all our heartfelt expressions of love, adoration and thanksgiving. High praises bring our sprits into the pinnacle of fellowship and intimacy between God and his children.

Praises magnifies our awareness of our spiritual union with the highest God, and transports us into the realm of the supernatural, which is in the presence of the power of the Almighty. Therefore when gratitude springs up in the human heart towards God, he is magnified as the wealthy source of our blessings and acknowledged as the giver and a glorious Father.

There are several actions involved in praising God. They can consist of verbal expression of adoration, praise and thanksgiving, singing, playing of instruments, dancing and lifting or clapping of hands. However, true praise is not merely going through these emotions.

Jesus spoke about the hypocrisy of the Pharisees, whose worships were only outward displays and lip service rather than indications of genuine expression of their love for the faithfulness of our living God. *'These people draweth nigh unto me with their mouths, and honoureth me with their lips, but their heart is far from me'* - **Matthew 15:8**

I have come to realized that a genuine praise to God is a matter of humility and sincere devotion to the Lord with true heart. And as the psalmist will say, *'enter into his gates with*

CHAPTER ELEVEN

thanksgiving, and into his courts with praise. Be thankful to him and bless his holy name, for the Lord is good' - **Psalms 100:4-5.**

The secret key is that if you ever want anything from God, you will have to thank and acknowledge him for what he has already provided; this is what is known as faith. The problem with us is that we are mostly very quick to ask God for his help, but slow to offer thanks unto him for what he so generously provides us. The Bible puts it succinctly with its account of the 10 lepers - Luke 17:17-18.

As we need deliverance, we would need to express thankfulness to the Lord for what he has already done. The book of Philippians 4.6 encourages us not to be anxious for nothing, but in everything by prayer and supplication, with thanksgiving, let our requests be known to God.

Praise to God is a Lifestyle. All too often, praise to God is something that many people leave in the church, as they see it as an event that should only happen when they come together in fellowship with other believers or Christians. However, praise should be a part and parcel of the believer's lifestyle and part of your daily prayer life - in the car, at home, in the kitchen, bedroom, bathroom, and indeed at all times and places. Praise to the Lord brings about the refreshing of His presence, along with his power and anointing. *'I will bless the Lord at all times, his praise shall continually be in my mouth'* - **Psalms 34:1**

CHAPTER ELEVEN

Praise is an expression of faith and a declaration of victory. It declares the believer's deep acknowledgement of his divine authority and sovereignty over all our circumstances – see Romans 8:28.

Praise is a 'sacrifice' that we offer to God voluntarily, for the faith we have in His being and for His abundance of kind mercies and grace but not just out of fun. *'By him therefore let us offer the sacrifice of praise to God continually, that is, the fruit of our lips giving thanks to his name'* - **Hebrews 13:15**

Your enemies are dealt with by God through praise. Since praise manifest God's presence, we must also realize that it repels the presence of the enemy, Satan. An atmosphere filled with sincere praise and worship of God by humble, devoted, committed and contrite hearts disgusts the devil. He fears, and will flee from, the power and the presence of the almighty God.

'Whoso offereth praise glorifieth me, and to him that ordereth his conversation all right will l show the salvation of God' - **Psalms 50:23**

When the children of Judah found themselves outnumbered by the hostile armies of Ammon and Moab at Mount Seir, King Jehoshaphat and all the people sought the Lord's help. The Lord assured the people that this would be his battle, and told them to go out against them, and that he would do the fighting for them.

So what did the children of Judah do? Being the people of

CHAPTER ELEVEN

'praise', given Judah actually means Praise, and knowing that God manifests his power through praise and worship, they sent their armies against the enemy, led by praise singers, declaring 'Praise the Lord, for his mercy endureth forever'. The consequences of their actions is well recorded in 2 Chronicles 20:22. When God's people begin to praise his name, it sends the enemy running.

I challenge you to become a person of praise and you will experience the release of the power of God in an awesome way. God gives us assurances of additional blessings as we praise him. When we praise God, He honours us as His children, provides His loving divine protection and divine covering – see 2 Samuel: 22: 47-51. Our failure to praise the Lord leaves us out of His loving divine protection and divine covering, hence we become exposed to the vagaries of the enemy – see 1 Samuel 2: 27-32.

You may be familiar with that wonderful and exciting chorus 'under the canopy of God'. If you do as I do, come along and begin to praise the great Jehovah now. May God richly bless you for this praise. Our praise can also serve as a testimony or witness to those who do not know the Lord – see 1 Peter 2:9; for the Lord our God works miraculously through praises.

Thankfulness encourages and motivates people. I recollect what my Bishop said during a thanksgiving meeting a little while ago, that 'thankfulness is contagious'. It is a fact of life that whatever we do sets example for other people. Thus if we fail to show a thankful heart to our God by our actions, we may become stumbling blocks to other people. This explains why believers need to demonstrate high degrees of commitment, devotion and seriousness of attitude during praise and worship sessions at all times.

Today in our church we have a devoted full service purposely for thanksgiving, praise and worship. The testimonies of this session are abundant; among others is the resulting regularization of the immigration status of those members of the congregation who placed their needs of indefinite leave to remain in the United Kingdom, before Almighty God.

We have set an atmosphere of praise and worship which impacts heavily on our new members and even first-time visitors, as they are able to testify to the lifting up of their spirits before the Lord and their feelings of being blessed. My personal testimony is the realization that when thanksgiving is practically demonstrated, such as evangelism, it blesses others and sets examples for those around us.

Thankfulness strengthens your faith. *'Rooted and built up in him and established in the faith, as ye have been taught, abounding therein with thanksgiving'* - **Colossians 2:7**

CHAPTER ELEVEN

Thanksgiving is so powerful that it lifts up your faith and encourages others. The word of God says that without faith it is impossible to please God. In this sense thankfulness may be seen as the fuel to faithfulness, as it strengthens the faith of the believer and his/her dependence on the Lord for all their provisions.

My Bishop says: 'God is all you need to have all your needs met adequately'. I could not agree more.

If you have been feeling defeated, it could be because you have forgotten the benefits of God through thanksgiving – see Habakkuk 3:17-18, Joel 1; 1-2, *'You shall know the truth and the truth shall set you free'*.

Let God's word tell you who you are and what you have. Don't give attention to anyone who tells you anything different, for God's word is true. When God called Gideon a mighty warrior, there was no evidence to suggest that it was true. God saw and spoke about what will become.

Learn and understand what God says about you and accept his opinion. Believe what God says about who you are in Christ Jesus, and you will become just what you are in Him. By faith through thanksgiving, believe the truth and act on what you believe. You will build your faith as you constantly remind yourself who you are in Christ Jesus.

CHAPTER ELEVEN

Thankfulness is the fuel that sustains your sure faith.

Develop the attitude to be thankful to God always, because thankful people always have their tanks full of God's blessings and divine favour. Begin to praise yourself into your destiny and know that praises break limitations.

CONCLUSION

What are your limitations? Have you been subject to personal limitations that hindered you from getting to your destiny? The good news is that you are above all limitations that prevented you from reaching that dream. Unless you tackle the limitations that appear to prevent you and your family through reading the word of God, engaging in fervent prayer, trusting in the Lord through faith, renewing your mindset and staying away from toxic relationships, it may be more difficult to move forward.

Interestingly, some people put up all sorts of barriers or limitations for themselves through fear, lack of confidence or simply lack of information. The Bible says 'Through lack of knowledge my people perished'. You were born for this time and nothing shall limit your destiny. And who knows whether you have come to the world for such a time as this? It is your time; it's your moment to cross over into your sure future. You could not have been relevant if you had showed up before now. Know that you have been divinely programmed to overcome all limitations and be a winner in this world.

Therefore do not allow the situations of life limit you. Stand on the solid word of God concerning you, take your place in the world and be relevant and significant to your generation.

No more limits to your destiny, as you discover yourself in the word of God and change your attitude about the way you see yourself, how you approach life's challenges and develop the attitude of thanksgiving. You cannot be limited anymore. Go, pursue and recover.

NO MORE LIMITS TO YOUR DESTINY.

Some inspirational quotes to motivate you:

'*Little minds are tamed and subdued by misfortune, but great minds rise above them*' - **Washington Irving**

It is when ordinary people rise above the expectations and seize the opportunity that milestones truly are reached'
- **Mike Huckabee**

'*It doesn't matter if a million people tell you what you can't do or if ten million tell you no, if you get one 'yes' from God that's all you need*' - **Tyler Perry**

'*Space is as infinite as we can imagine, and expanding this perspective is what adjusts humankind's focus and limitations*'
- **VannaBonta**

'*Limitations live only in our minds, but if we use our imaginations our possibilities become limitless*'
- **Jamie Paolinetti**

'Success is not final. Failure is not fatal, it is the courage to continue that counts' - **Winston Churchill**

'All the concepts about stepping out of your comfort zone mean nothing until you decide that your essential purpose, vision and goals are more important than your self-imposed limitations'
- **Robert White**

'If you stay focused and right on track, you will get to where you want to be.' - **unknown**

'Trust yourself. You know more than you think you do'
- **Benjamin Spock, MD**

'There's no better place to search for hope than the future; a concept that gives everyone in existence a reason to live.'
- **Amy Newak**

BIBLIOGRAPHY

Books by Bishop Michael Hutton-Wood
Leadership capsules
I shall rise again
How to negotiate your desired future with today's currency
You need to do the ridiculous to experience the miraculous
175 reasons why you cannot fail
What to do in the darkest hour of your trail
Leadership secrets
Leadership nuggets
Taking the struggle out of ministry

Books by David O. Abioye
Productive thinking
Overcoming stagnation

Books by Dr David Oyedepo
Understanding vision
In pursuit of vision
Maximize destiny
All you need to have all your needs met
Divine direction
Exploit in ministry

Rhonda Jones
You must change your mind to change your life

Mary Whelchel
Defeating discouragement

Lester Sumrall
Making life count

R W Schambach
What to do when trouble comes

E M Bound
The weapon of prayer

Gordon Lindsay
Prayer that moves mountains

BOOKS AND LEADERSHIP MANUALS
BY BISHOP MICHAEL HUTTON-WOOD

| What is Ministry | My Daily Bible Reading Guide | Leadership Nuggets | 175 Reasons Why You Cannot And Will Not Fail In Life |

| I Shall Rise Agian | Leadership Capsules | What To Do In The Darkest Hour of Your Trial | Generating Finances For Ministry |

TRAINING MANUALS FOR IMPACTFUL LEADERSHIP & EFFECTIVE MINISTRY

Please log on to www.houseofjudah.org.uk for more information

OTHER BOOKS BY THE AUTHOR
- BISHOP MICHAEL HUTTON-WOOD -

Why You Should Pray for your Pastor And For Your Church Daily

200 Questions You Must Ask, Investigate And Know Before You Say I Do

A Must For Every New Convert

How To Negotiate Your Desired Future With Today's Currency

Leadership Secrets

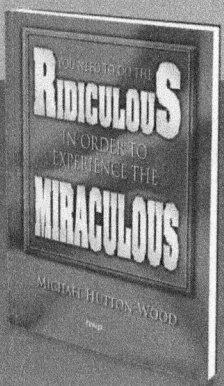
You Need To Do The Ridiculous In Order To Experience The Miraculous

Please log on to
www.houseofjudah.org.uk for more information

www.ingramcontent.com/pod-product-compliance
Lightning Source LLC
Chambersburg PA
CBHW071703040426
42446CB00011B/1890